"Here's a pastor-theologian God refuses to be God without us. In these rich, lyrical meditations, Travis Jamieson testifies—not with doctrinal pronouncements but with doxology. He draws on a wide cast of writers, saints, scholars, and fellow strugglers in faith to show us the joy, the strange delight, of believing. Whether you're just beginning the journey of faith or limping along somewhere in the middle, Travis will give you good company and strong encouragement for the road."

—Will Willimon, Professor of the Practice of Christian Ministry, Duke Divinity School

"In a world of deconstructing faith, Travis Jamieson offers a word of hope. Jamieson's book does not offer simplistic answers—but rather bears witness to the truth that there is a pure simplicity on the far side of complexity. Jamieson weaves together a wide array of sources—from Augustine to Calvin to Wendell Berry to Dostoevsky to Yuval Harari and beyond—to show how the Christian faith still answers the deepest questions of life. This is a winsome and thoughtful book, a good introduction to the essence of the Christian faith."

—Gerald Hiestand, Senior Pastor, Calvary Memorial Church

"In a time when portraits of Jesus are commodified and coopted, Travis Jamieson gives us a humane, theologically rich, and engaging introduction to the one who died, was raised, and will come again. He weaves together Scripture, personal testimony, literature, and theologians of the past in a manner that is both welcoming and reliable. This is a terrific introduction to life in Christ."

—Fellipe do Vale, Assistant Professor of Biblical and Systematic Theology, Trinity Evangelical Divinity School

"Travis Jamieson writes with simplicity and depth—a potent combination. Centering his book where the Bible does, Jamieson presents a compelling account of Jesus Christ in a story that is forever old and forever new. You would have to be numb not to be moved by it."

—CORNELIUS PLANTINGA, author of *Morning and Evening Prayers*

"In *The Mystery of Faith*, Travis Jamieson invites us into a profound yet simple exploration of the unexplainable truth of Christ. Rather than solving the mystery, he guides us toward the person of Christ. Through accessible theological reflection, personal stories, contemporary authors, and relevant examples, we are led on a journey through Christ's life, death, resurrection, and return. The outcome is a compelling appeal for the timeless beauty of the gospel."

—PAUL TAYLOR, Co-Founder, Bay Area Center for Faith, Work & Tech

# The Mystery of Faith

# The Mystery of Faith

## Why the Gospel Is Still Good News

TRAVIS JAMIESON

*Foreword by* GARY M. BURGE

WIPF & STOCK • Eugene, Oregon

THE MYSTERY OF FAITH
Why the Gospel Is Still Good News

Copyright © 2025 Travis Jamieson. All rights reserved. Except for brief quotations in critical publications or reviews, no part of this book may be reproduced in any manner without prior written permission from the publisher. Write: Permissions, Wipf and Stock Publishers, 199 W. 8th Ave., Suite 3, Eugene, OR 97401.

Wipf & Stock
An Imprint of Wipf and Stock Publishers
199 W. 8th Ave., Suite 3
Eugene, OR 97401

www.wipfandstock.com

PAPERBACK ISBN: 979-8-3852-3311-3
HARDCOVER ISBN: 979-8-3852-3312-0
EBOOK ISBN: 979-8-3852-3313-7

All Scripture quotations, unless otherwise indicated, are taken from the Holy Bible, New International Version®, NIV®. Copyright ©1973, 1978, 1984, 2011 by Biblica, Inc.™ Used by permission of Zondervan. All rights reserved worldwide. www.zondervan.com The "NIV" and "New International Version" are trademarks registered in the United States Patent and Trademark Office by Biblica, Inc.™

*To those I hold most dear: Annie, Cecilia, and Abel*

# Contents

Foreword by Gary M. Burge  ix
Acknowledgments  xi
Introduction: The Mystery of Faith  xiii

PART 1: CHRIST HAS DIED
Created for Life  3
Tempted by Death  10
Saved Through Death  18

PART 2: CHRIST IS RISEN
Death Is Defeated  33
Life Is Secure  45
Love Is Guaranteed  55

PART 3: CHRIST WILL COME AGAIN
The Spirit Is with Us  67
Our Flesh Is in God's Presence  75
Judgment Is a Comfort  84

Conclusion: All Things Made New  93
Bibliography  97

# Foreword

EVERY GENERATION NEEDS TO reexamine the fundamentals of its Christian faith and express them once more for a new era and a new audience. A long list of names including writers from G. K. Chesterton to R. C. Sproul and Michael Bird—the list could be very long—each have written passionately about the essence of the Christian faith and the fundamental convictions that help us remember why we believe and what we believe. Each comes from a different context, serving people in a variety of traditions. C. S. Lewis's *Mere Christianity* and N. T. Wright's *Simply Christian: Why Christianity Makes Sense* are likely the two most prominent today.

This writing has a rich Christian tradition and Travis Jamieson belongs to it, writing for a new generation. *The Mystery of Faith* is a blend of personal narrative, confessional outline, and apologia (though Travis would hesitate at this last label). His is an exploration of the mystery of faith that every sincere believer embraces. In other words, when we step into the historic faith of the church, we are joining an entire way of thinking and believing as we live our lives in this world. It is this system, with its many stories, creeds, and practices, that shapes how we view the world. It is part logic and part mystery, but this is the balance that each of us brings to any worldview we hold sincerely: reason and mystery. Travis is here simply bringing into clarity the milestones of thinking and believing that make up the deep structures of our Christian belief system.

His organizing framework is the ancient liturgical confession: "Christ has died, Christ is risen, Christ will come again."

## Foreword

This timeless triple confession appears in the Eucharist liturgies of many traditions and today is almost universally celebrated. It is anchored to the remembrance words of Jesus in the upper room during his final meal. We are called to remember Jesus' death, his resurrection, and anticipate his coming again. These three beliefs are the pillars anchoring the Christian belief system, and understanding them clearly is Travis's goal.

His inspiration for this effort was watching one of his former pastors, a mentor and leader for years, suddenly quit his role as pastor and then deconstruct everything about what he believed. In a podcast interview in 2023, this former pastor not only disagreed with Christian faith but said that he and his wife were repelled by it. "The gospel is not good news," he announced.[1] A proclaimer of the gospel suddenly had become one of its opponents; a leader whose life had shaped and helped many (including Travis) had now become a defector from the ranks of the faithful.

This book is Travis's eloquent, passionate explanation of what his mentor had given up. In one sense this book is ironic. The student, taught as a youth by his pastor, now is explaining the very faith his pastor has abandoned. Travis-the-student has now become Travis-the-teacher—and one wonders, one hopes, that his former pastor will find this book and see what he has discarded.

Travis's work is part storytelling and part theological musings at the highest level. He can talk about his childhood as easily as he can cite Karl Barth, Richard Mouw, Henri Nouwen, Cornelius Plantinga, Walter Brueggemann, or Brené Brown. That is, Travis can artfully explain the complex at multiple levels, bringing a brilliant simplicity to his explanations that only a skilled pastor/theologian can do.

This is a presentation of our faith for a new and younger generation. It is well grounded theologically, alert to nuance, and profound in all of the right ways. We are in Travis's debt for all that he has done here.

Gary M. Burge, PhD
Calvin Theological Seminary (retired)

1. Mahon, *Slow Train*.

# Acknowledgments

I'M GRATEFUL TO GOD for the many people he has placed in my life who encouraged me to write this book. First and foremost, thanks to my wife, Annie, for supporting me through all the ups and downs of my writing journey. You have always been my biggest fan and have believed in me even when I didn't believe in myself. Your continuous encouragement throughout the writing process is a key reason this book exists today. Thank you to my children, Cecilia and Abel; you both serve as daily reminders of God's abundant love in my life. I appreciate my congregation at Palo Alto Christian Reformed Church for being a place where the good news of the gospel can be proclaimed in both word and deed. I have witnessed how much of what this book conveys has been embodied by you as we've grown to know each other over the past few years. I'm thankful to Gary Burge for inspiring me to write; you have never once doubted my abilities. Instead, you've been a steadfast companion of grace and love. I hope every writer has a Gary Burge in their corner. I am especially grateful for Marcus Johnson's systematic theology classes at Moody Bible Institute, where I learned that the gospel is not merely an abstract message; it is a person, specifically, Jesus Christ. Much of what is included in this book is a direct result of what I learned in those classes. Thank you, Jen Baham, for editing some of the earlier chapter drafts. Finally, thank you to Nathaniel Schmidt for pointing me toward Wipf and Stock and for rooting for me throughout the writing process.

# Introduction: The Mystery of Faith

*My goal is that they may be encouraged in heart and united in love, so that they may have the full riches of complete understanding, so that they may know the mystery of God, namely, Christ, in whom are hidden all the treasures of wisdom and knowledge.*

COLOSSIANS 2:2–3

*Life is not something we manage to hammer together and keep in repair by our wits; it is an unfathomable gift. We are immersed in mysteries: incredible love, confounding evil, the creation, the cross, grace, God.*

EUGENE PETERSON, *THE CONTEMPLATIVE PASTOR*

AS AN EIGHT-YEAR-OLD BOY, I remember peering at ten middle-aged male elders across six burgundy padded pews as they prepared to serve the bread and cup. They always gave me the impression that the Lord's Supper was a serious matter. Before the elders passed out the bread and the cup to the congregation, one of them gave a homily encouraging us to make amends with our brothers and sisters in Christ. As I looked down the pew at my ten brothers and sisters, I knew he meant my real brothers and sisters, too. He continued and said, "If we are not at peace with one another, then we are eating and drinking judgment on ourselves." I felt the pressure land on me like a two-ton anvil. I'm all for making amends and living at peace with other church members, but this threat of judgment left me feeling as anxious as a dog in a thunderstorm.

Fast forward twenty years. I'm looking over a sea of people sitting in grey chairs and listening to Pastor Karen, adorned with white robes, as she holds up her arms in the shape of a cross and recites the mystery of faith, "Christ has died, Christ is risen, Christ will come again." A simple yet profound summary of the Christian faith: it's not about what you've done but what Jesus did. No sermon about making things right with everyone around me. No worries about God's judgment. Just an unapologetic call to Christ. Instead of asking my youth's "what if" questions and feeling stressed about my eternal destiny, I'm filled with joy.

The difference between these two experiences at the table revolved around who was at the center of attention. In my childhood memory, I looked inward, and I was overwhelmed with anxiety. My stomach twisted into knots. It was like a dark cloud eclipsed the joy of sunshine. In my adult years, as I waited for the bread and the cup, I was directed outwards, away from myself and toward Jesus. Yes, the apostle Paul's command to live at peace with all people still applied, but I knew who the source of peace was this time. Peace would never be found in confessing every last sin in my life. Peace would only be found in the God who became flesh and dwelt among us, the God who made peace by the blood of the cross, the God who conquered the grave, the God who became our eternal and righteous high priest and sent his Spirit to make a home within us.

The exact words used in the liturgy are, "After supper he took the cup of wine; and when he had given thanks, he gave it to them, and said, 'Drink this, all of you: This is my blood of the new covenant, which is shed for you and for many for the forgiveness of sins. Whenever you drink it, do this for the remembrance of me.' Therefore, we proclaim the mystery of faith: *Christ has died. Christ is risen. Christ will come again.*" Christians have always confessed that Jesus, the Son of God, coeternal with the Father and the Spirit, came to this world, took on flesh, and suffered so that evil might be defeated and people might be forgiven of their sins. Christians

## Introduction: The Mystery of Faith

believe that the same Jesus who is God and who died didn't stay dead. He came back to life, ate breakfast with his disciples, and taught them about the kingdom of God. Then, to think it could not get more impressive, Christians believe that Jesus ascended back to the Father's right hand in heaven after forty days. From there, he is the mediator and great high priest and will one day come to judge the living and the dead. Christians believe we are nourished spiritually by Jesus, through the power of the Holy Spirit, in the bread and the wine of the Lord's Supper.

This mystery of Jesus Christ is the center of the Christian faith. Without him, Christianity would not exist. Yet, like all mysteries, the mysterious nature of the person and work of Jesus can be mistaken as a mystery needing to be solved. Instead of bowing down and worshiping such a profound reality, the twenty-first-century mind is geared toward eliminating mystery for the sake of certainty. As a result, many Christians have walked away from the faith because they have become dissatisfied with or even offended by the answers they've received to their many questions.

This process of questioning one's faith is known as deconstruction. Our cultural norms praise and even expect young adults to deconstruct the faith of their childhood. As I grew into adulthood, I, too, deconstructed much of what I had learned about Christianity, the Bible, and God. Deconstruction is an essential process of growing up in one's faith. I needed to shed some of the narratives I was taught as a child because they were meant to be for children. I needed to learn narratives to help me live out my faith as an adult. As I did, I realized how little I knew about the Christian faith and how I often found more questions than answers. When I was introduced to the concept of mystery and the centrality it holds within the Christian faith during my college years, I learned that I didn't need to run from my faith when I had questions and doubts, but rather, I could dive deeper into the bottomless well that is God the Father, the Son, and the Holy Spirit revealed to believers in the Holy Scriptures.

However, deconstructionism can also lead people to abandon their faith in Jesus completely. My childhood pastor is one example of many. Pastor Matt taught me the gospel of Jesus. He exemplified what it meant to love Jesus and others and even inspired me to pursue pastoral ministry. Yet, several years into my journey toward pastoring, I was surprised to hear that Matt had left the ministry. We had lost touch over the years, so I didn't know the details, but I assumed that, like many burned-out pastors, he was ready for a change. Church work is not easy. He was always a man of integrity and a strong leader, so it didn't surprise me when I heard later on that he was drawn to law enforcement. However, a few years later, I heard an interview he did on a podcast focused on the process of deconstruction. He and his wife, Mandy, told their story. They explained that the more they studied and understood the Christian faith, the more they felt repelled by it, especially by the idea that their upstanding non-Christian neighbors would not be going to heaven. They described their neighbors as better people than themselves, so how could they accept a belief system that damned them to hell. As Matt's deconstruction continued, he came to a surprising conclusion: "The gospel is not good news."[1] Those six words shocked me, and I've been wrestling with them ever since. Is the gospel still good news?

Whether you are in the middle of your deconstruction journey, know someone who is, or are just looking to wrestle deeply with the mystery of faith, this book is for you. This book explores the centrality of the Christian faith: "Christ has died, Christ is risen, Christ will come again." This book is not an apologetic work. It does not try to defend the faith. The mystery of faith is not a problem that needs to be solved. Instead, think of this book as a lantern that shines a bit of light down a long pathway. We may not know every nook and cranny of the path, but as we put one step in front of the other, we will see new aspects of the path and learn more about where it is leading us. Contemplating the mystery of faith helps us grow in understanding and learn to worship the Author of this mystery anew so that wherever you are on your faith journey, you'll be reminded of who Jesus is, why he came to this world, and why he is good news for you.

1. Mahon, *Slow Train*.

# PART 1: CHRIST HAS DIED

# 1

# Created for Life

*Then the LORD God formed a man from the dust of the ground and breathed into his nostrils the breath of life, and the man became a living being.*

Genesis 2:7

*He who commits his life to this son of man does not die, but he who does not commit his life to him destroys himself by not trusting to what is life itself. Division (death) consists in this, that life came into the world, but men go away from that life.*

Leo Tolstoy, *Gospel in Brief*

I FELT THE VIBRANCY of life flow through me like a thread through a needle as I stood in front of that group of strangers in my navy suit, white shirt, and black wing tips. It's not the feeling I expected as I officiated that funeral. Yet, that sea of faces gathered in an old Baptist church in rural Michigan did not just come to grieve. They came to remember. John had died just days before. He had been a staple in their community for decades, but most hadn't seen him in years because he had moved away to be closer to his kids. So, as they gathered to grieve his death, they also gathered to remember his life. They remembered when he showed up to help organize the state fair, met them for coffee on their farms, and worshiped God with them at church. They remembered his corny jokes, warm laugh, and kind blue eyes. I remembered the day before he died when I read to him the psalmist's words, "I lift up my eyes to the hills—where does my help come from? My help comes from the LORD, the Maker of heaven and earth."[1] As we looked to God for help amid death, we remembered that John was created for life.

Without John's life, finding much meaning in his death would have been difficult. Without a lifetime of touching so many others with his generosity and care, there wouldn't have been a crowd of people gathered to reminisce. Without his lived reality, there would be no need to ponder what came after his death.

The same goes for the death of Christ. To find meaning in Jesus' death, we must first understand why he had to enter into this life. Through his death, he took the penalty of sins, but why was a penalty necessary in the first place? Jesus came into this world to save sinners. What made sinners need to be saved? He became the once and for all blood sacrifice for sins. Why was blood the required sacrifice for sins? He defeated the great enemy of death. Why is death our greatest enemy? He assured us we could be forgiven and live forever. Why is life eternal so worthwhile?

The answers to these questions are summed up in one phrase: *God created humanity for life with him.* Death was not supposed to be a part of the narrative. We were meant to enjoy God forever. Sin changed that. Death disrupted it. So, God went on a mission to bring us back into that life with him. As the Swiss theologian Karl Barth said,

> To put it in the simplest way, *what unites God and us men is that He does not will to be God without us*, that He creates us rather to share with us and therefore with our being and life and act His own incomparable being and life and act, *that He does not allow His history to be His and ours ours, but causes them to take place as a common*

1. Ps 121:1–2.

*history.* That is the special truth which the Christian message has to proclaim at its very heart.[2]

God refuses to be who he is apart from us, and it all begins in creation.

## GOD'S RELATIONAL CREATIVITY

God reveals himself in all that he makes and shows the world who he is. In utter darkness, the light of life appears. From a single-celled organism to birds with seven-foot wingspans, God's light shines forth through his creatures. From the unending chasm of space to over three hundred and fifty thousand varieties of beetles, God shows us his vastness and creativity. From the power of the sun to the vulnerability of a fawn, God reveals his mighty and gentle strength. Yet, amid all of his diverse creations, God found it to be lacking something that he wanted expressed more fully. So, he created one final species: humanity. This species, which included a man and a woman, was unlike anything else in the world. They were made in God's image.[3] They were created for union with him, and therefore, they were designed for eternal life.

God endowed his image-bearers with the responsibility of reflecting God's nature into the created world around them. Like a mirror reflects an image, humanity reflects God for all the world to see. Since God is Creator, humanity reflects his image as little creators. Since the apostle John defined God as "love,"[4] humanity reflects his image as little lovers in the world. This love looked a lot like work as Adam and Eve cared for and cultivated the garden, but with each vine they pruned, each row of tomatoes they planted, they were putting God's relational creativity on display.

If the very essence of God is love, then everything he does flows out of love. Love is the posture from which all God's actions move. Michael Reeves's book *Delighting in the Trinity* argues that

---

2. Barth, *CD* 4/1:7, emphasis added.
3. Gen 1:27.
4. 1 John 4:8.

God's act of creation flows out of his love. God did not create out of a sense of duty or need. As the supreme being, God has no duty to anyone beyond himself. If he reported to someone higher than himself, then he wouldn't be God. Likewise, because he is all powerful, he has no needs that he cannot fulfill himself. Therefore, duty and need were not motivating factors in creation. Instead, because God is triune as Father, Son, and Holy Spirit, all of creation proceeded from the deep and abiding love the Father has for the Son and the Spirit; the Son, for the Father and the Spirit; and the Spirit, for the Father and the Son. Imagine pouring a glass of water until it overflows. Eventually, the water source will run dry. With God, if his love is the water, it can overflow forever and never run dry because he is love and he is everlasting.

As God's love overflows, he shares it. There is no scarcity with God. He doesn't lose anything by giving his love away. Love is never a zero-sum game for him. Instead, he generously shares his love and is filled up all the more. He created humanity in his image so they might share in his unending love and reflect it to everything around them. God's love longs to be made real in true and lasting relationships between God and his creation. Essayist and novelist Wendell Berry writes in an essay entitled *Word and Flesh*, "Love is never abstract . . . It longs for incarnation."[5] This relational quality may be why some theologians argue that the image of God is fully expressed in a community rather than as an individual. In Richard Mouw's memoir, *Adventures in Evangelical Civility*, he writes about Herman Bavinck's theology of the image of God.[6] Bavinck argued that the image of God will be fully known when people of every tribe, nation, and tongue come together to worship in the throne room of God. In other words, we need one another to fully reflect who God is.

---

5. Berry, *What Are People For?*, 200.
6. Mouw, *Adventures*, 31.

## UNION WITH GOD

As Father, Son, and Holy Spirit, God is in perfect union within himself. Therefore, humanity reflects his nature by being united with God and the rest of his creation. Humankind is unique because of our relationship with the divine. Only humans interact with God, sin against him, and are punished or rewarded by him. Although there were many creatures in the garden of Eden, God only invited one species into a conversation. Herman Bavinck once wrote, "Life is the full, rich existence of man in the union of his soul and body, *in union with God* and in harmony with the world."[7] Bavinck concluded that life in a relationship with God is not some addition to the good life. Instead, it is the essence of the good life we long for. It is the very reason why we exist.

This union with God came as a result of his overflowing love. His love was the foundation for his willingness to humble himself and meet us on earth. Sociologist and researcher Brené Brown writes, "We cultivate love when we allow our most vulnerable and powerful selves to be deeply seen and known, and when we honor the spiritual connection that grows from that offering with trust, respect, kindness, and affection."[8] By creating out of his overflowing love, God became knowable. He opened himself up to humanity in actual vulnerability so we might know his power, love, and grace. As he became knowable, he invited us into a union of trust, respect, kindness, and affection. We need this kind of union from those who love us most, and God has promised to be this for us eternally.

God made us in his image and vulnerably became united with us because he created us for eternal life. Eternal life is first and foremost about becoming more united to God. Jesus said in John 17:3, "Now this is eternal life: that they know you, the only true God, and Jesus Christ, whom you have sent." The Greek word for "know" is not only about a piece of intellectual knowledge but also about an all-encompassing knowledge.[9] It's the kind of knowledge

---

7. Bavinck, *Guidebook*, 178, emphasis added.
8. Brown, *Gifts of Imperfection*, 35.
9. Burge, *John*, 463.

of another person a couple has after sixty years of marriage. If it's been a strong marriage, then this couple will know everything about each other and have shared the intimacy of a marriage bed for decades. Jesus wants to know us fully and be known by us fully and has designed eternal life to be for that purpose. He looks forward to the day when sin will no longer keep us at a distance; instead, we will be able to enjoy an intimacy unlike anything we have experienced before.

God's knowledge of us and our knowledge of him sets him apart from all idols. Idols made by human hands can't know their maker. Idols are made of wood, steel, or, more often, dreams, ambitions, achievements, and relationships. Idols are God's good gifts that have replaced the lordship of Jesus Christ in our lives. Paul writes in 1 Cor 8:4, "We know that 'An idol is nothing at all in the world' and that 'There is no God but one.'" An idol can do nothing, but the one God of our Lord Jesus Christ created this world and all that is in it. He is the one who deserves our praise, adoration, and devotion because he is the only God who can honestly know us.

A secure connection with this God is life's surest foundation. He is the God who was, who is, and who forever shall be. Nothing can overpower or overwhelm him. In twelve-step recovery groups, people with addictions encourage each other with the phrase, "Connection is the opposite of addiction." It's a simple yet profound truth that people are far less likely to turn to destructive habits when they have deep connections with God, others, and themselves. What is it about the connection that turns people away from addiction? From a biblical perspective, God created us for eternal life in union with him and the rest of creation. When we turn away from that union, life becomes unmanageable. Like a flame deprived of oxygen, we become a lesser version of ourselves without connection. Yet, when we lean into that connection, we become exactly who God created us to be and know the purpose for which we exist. Because God is immovable, he will always be there when we reach out to him.

Life-giving relationships are the bedrock of our shared humanity. That's why twelve-step groups like Alcoholics Anonymous exist. They don't offer some miraculous solution to addiction, but they offer an unconditional loving community and a guide to reconnecting with God, others, and oneself. As Jesus says in John 15:5, "I am the vine; you are the branches. If you remain in me and I in you, you will bear much fruit; apart from me, you can do nothing." The connection between God and humanity is essential to thriving because God is the source of all life. We must remain connected to the source or become deprived of what we need most.

## CONCLUSION

At John's funeral, the honor guard, made up of military veterans in meticulously pressed uniforms, concluded the service with a three-volley salute. As a young man, John had worn a uniform himself. He served in the military, and the honor guard remembered that service in his death. Before the service members lifted their rifles to fire three blank rounds into the blue sky, with all those touched by John's life gathered around, the service members slowly folded the American flag that draped John's coffin and carefully presented it to his widow. John finished his race, and his widow was commissioned to keep his memories alive and share them with others. As witnesses to John's life, all of us were called to live in light of our memories of John.

Most importantly though, we were called to live in light of John's faithful service to Jesus Christ. Even though we live east of Eden, we are still called to wave God's flag, not in an imperial kind of way, but in a celebrative way. We are God's image-bearers, his reflection, his ambassadors. As such, we are honored with the duty of making his name known through our words and actions. Though we fall short of this calling, we continually look to Jesus, who never fell short. Jesus raised God's flag and never let go so that one day, we might experience union with God without the hindrance of sin. Jesus needed to die to end death because we were created for eternal life, knowing God, and being known by him. Jesus won't rest until we experience the life we were created for.

# 2

# Tempted by Death

*When tempted, no one should say, "God is tempting me." For God cannot be tempted by evil, nor does he tempt anyone; but each person is tempted when they are dragged away by their own evil desire and enticed. Then, after desire has conceived, it gives birth to sin; and sin, when it is full-grown, gives birth to death.*

JAMES 1:13–15

*What makes the temptation of power so seemingly irresistible? Maybe it is that power offers an easy substitute for the hard task of love. It seems easier to be God than to love God, easier to control people than to love people, easier to own life than to love life.*

HENRI NOUWEN, *IN THE NAME OF JESUS*

GOD CREATED US FOR life, but we know from experience and the biblical narrative that death plagues us. As I write this, the news of war and civilian death is on all the major news outlets and social media feeds. The Middle East is in chaos. Russia continues to invade Ukraine. The war continues in Sudan. There appears to be no end in sight to the violence and loss of life. Of course, we don't have to look at the news to know death is among us. My church sits two doors down from a cemetery. Although the grass is green, the headstones perfectly aligned, and the pathways swept, the stench of death is eerily present. Some of those buried there, like Steve Jobs and Shirley Temple, seem to live on eternally in our cultural narrative, yet they are just as dead as the names that no one knows or remembers. Death is the destiny of all people of all time.

The destiny of death threatens to disrupt peace and throw life into chaos at any moment. I was sitting at our dining room table, surrounded by family and friends, when I bit into my rice and meat, only to begin choking a moment later. I didn't know what was happening, so I stood up, walked around the corner to the kitchen, and tried spitting the food into the sink. As the seconds ticked on, I realized I could not catch my breath. I couldn't talk. Panic set in. I thought this might be the end. Then, I felt my wife's hands around my gut. The food came launching out of my throat and into the sink. I could breathe again! I sat back down at our dining table, but I couldn't focus, the sudden threat of death rattled me.

To better understand the death of Jesus, we need to explore why death plagues humanity. His death intrinsically connects to our deaths and vice versa. Therefore, as we understand what leads to our deaths, why death is God's punishment for sin, and how death continues to be our greatest temptation, we lay the groundwork for a deeper engagement with Jesus' death.

## FROM SHALOM TO CHAOS

If God created us for life, it was for a life marked by shalom. According to Cornelius Plantinga, author of a classic book on the doctrine of sin, shalom is "the webbing together of God, humans, and all creation in justice, fulfillment, and delight. . . .

## The Mystery of Faith

In other words, shalom is the way things ought to be."[1] In the story of the Bible, the garden of Eden was an incubator for shalom. Eden represents a paradise that we all desire, a place where pain, misery, and injustice find no foothold and peace reigns supreme. It's why my Jewish neighbor greets me on Sundays with the words "Shabbat Shalom," which translates to "peace on the Sabbath." She's hoping that during my day of rest, I get a taste of how things were supposed to be before sin entered the world. In other words, she is praying that I reconnect with God, humanity, and all of creation.

As Adam and Eve roamed the garden, caring for the plants and naming the animals, everything they could need was within arms reach. They ate a juicy assortment of fruits and vegetables with colors that spanned that of the rainbow. Water, pure enough to drink straight from the river, was always available on tap. They even walked side by side with their Creator God along the garden's paths lined with apricot and orange trees. Yet, this bliss was short-lived before the slimy snake caught Eve's attention. He began to woo her with dreams of something more than what she could see, something more than just a juicy apple. He tempted her with the knowledge that she could be God. Orthodox priest Alexander Schmemann explains, "The 'original' sin is not primarily that man has 'disobeyed' God; the sin is that he ceased to be hungry for Him and for Him alone, ceased to see his whole life depending on the whole world as a sacrament of communion with God."[2] Everything in Adam and Eve's habitat gave them a means to commune with their Creator. By believing the snake's lie that God was holding back something from them, they became possessed by a craving for something more.

God hates sin because it disrupts the peace in which God meant creation to exist. Sin fractures the relationships between humans and God, humans and other humans, and humans and the rest of creation. When Adam and Eve took what the snake had to offer, they turned away from shalom and toward chaos and death.

---

1. Plantinga, *Not the Way*, 10.
2. Schmemann, *For the Life*, 18.

Plantinga defines sin as the "culpable disturbance of shalom."[3] After sin enters shalom, once content, Adam and Eve feel shame and hide from the One who loves them unconditionally.

The spiritual union that Adam and Eve experienced with God in the garden ended when they sinned. The intimate connection they once had with God was no more. Their relationship went from being marked by joy-filled love to being marked by shame-filled fear. Death entered into their lives and wreaked chaos in their relationship with God. "Sin is the smearing of a relationship, the grieving of one's divine parent and benefactor, a betrayal of the partner to whom one is joined by a holy bond."[4] As children estranged from their parents, Adam and Eve lost their most important connection. Their desire for more than what God had provided undermined the security they once felt with God watching over them. As their quickness to blame shows, they no longer could trust one another and must have felt utterly alone for the first time. They use the beauty of leaves to cover their shame and begin turning on one another as soon as God asks what happened. It's the beginning of a long exile away from shalom, away from what God intended for his people. Genesis 3:23–24 reads (emphasis added),

> So the Lord God *banished* him from the Garden of Eden to work the ground from which he had been taken. After he *drove* the man out, he placed on the east side of the Garden of Eden cherubim and a flaming sword flashing back and forth to guard the way to the tree of life.

Adam and Eve would never return to their habitat of shalom.

Sin also caused a crack in the relationship between humanity and the earth. Creation becomes Adam and Eve's enemy. Instead of enjoying the task of caring for and cultivating the garden, the soil becomes rocky, sandy, and challenging to work with. Years of drought, too much rain, and human limitations make farming some of our most difficult work. Walter Brueggemann writes, "The

---

3. Plantinga, *Not the Way*, 16.
4. Plantinga, *Not the Way*, 12.

sentence is life apart from the goodness of the garden, life in conflict filled with pain, with sweat, and most interestingly, with the distortion of desire."[5] What was once a joy, became a drudgery. The Sunday evening blues took over and the eternal wait for Friday began.

## THE NATURE OF TEMPTATION

So, the question becomes, why do humans turn away from shalom and toward death? If God offers Adam and Eve everything they need, if they know true peace in the garden, why would they ever put themselves at risk of losing it? It's a tricky question to answer. Returning to the story of temptation in Gen 3, we can glean a few clues as to why death tempts them.

The temptation begins with a clever voice questioning God's word. The serpent was the craftiest creature in the garden. In ancient Near Eastern communities, the snake was considered wise and associated with death. Like the best marketers and salespeople, the serpent was an expert in convincing others to do what he wanted them to do. He doesn't start the conversation with Eve by telling her to rebel against her Creator. Instead, he catches her attention by saying something obviously untrue. "Did God say, 'You must not eat from any tree in the garden?'"[6] Eve replied, "We may eat fruit from the trees in the garden, but God did say, 'You must not eat fruit from the tree that is in the middle of the garden, and you must not touch it, or you will die.'"[7] By this point, the serpent has subtly hooked Eve like a fish on the end of a lure. Eve was deep into an encounter with the devil and didn't even know it. And that's when he knows he has her. He comes into full force and denies what God said. "You will not certainly die. For God knows that when you eat from it your eyes will be opened, and you will be

---

5. Brueggemann, *Genesis*, 50.
6. Gen 3:1.
7. Gen 3:2–3.

like God, knowing good and evil."[8] The serpent deceptively denies what God said about the consequence of death, and then he offers something new: "You will be like God." Who can pass this up? If death is not actually a threat and becoming divine is possible, then why wouldn't Eve take and eat?

The Genesis account describes Eve's temptation sensually. It begins with taste. After the serpent seduces her into giving the forbidden fruit a second thought, she sees it as "good for food."[9] The desire for food is as essential to humanity as barking is for dogs. I can barely go a few hours without thinking about my next snack or meal. Yet, a bountiful garden surrounded Eve. She didn't need this one fruit to survive. If anything, the forbidden fruit was an excess. It's like eating an extra piece of cake. It tastes good, but you know you don't need it. You know it's terrible for you. Before her casual conversation with the serpent, she considered the fruit off-limits, but now her mind has changed. She sees it as good. And that's how temptation undermines our spiritual senses. It transforms bad into good. By the time Eve bit into that delicious fruit, she had completely forgotten God's warnings and was engulfed in the serpent's lie.

However, it wasn't just the taste that convinced Eve to eat the fruit. There was another sense at play. The fruit looked good. The fruit captivated her eyes, like when you hike a trail, start to feel fatigued, round the next bend, look across the glowing field ahead of you, and see a colorful bow hanging in the sky. Rainbows stop us in our tracks and create a sense of awe in our hearts. Perhaps that's what happened with Eve. Once she accepted that the forbidden fruit wasn't forbidden, its glorious splendor altered her vision. She stood in awe of creation instead of the Creator. Her eyes deceived her.

Finally, with her mouth watering and her eyes glued to the fruit, she fully accepted the devil's lie that the fruit would make her wise. Instead of trusting in God for insights and guidance, Eve would be a self-made woman. Like the wicked queen in Snow

---

8. Gen 3:4.
9. Gen 3:6.

White, Eve can imagine eating the fruit, looking at her reflection, and saying, "Who is the wisest of them all?" to which her reflection responds, "You are." Eve and, by extension, Adam would become the most powerful creatures on earth. Ironically, they are already God's most intelligent creatures. The fruit is not just about becoming the wisest creature but becoming like God. The fruit represented the desire to rule over the Creator. It was a revolutionary act, an attack on their king.

At this point, theologian Michael Horton helpfully articulates what Adam and Eve are doing by sinning against God. He argues that, like a court employing witnesses to build a case, Adam and Eve became false witnesses against God. Instead of being God's witnesses of truth, they became false witnesses seeking to turn the world against him. Horton puts it this way, "Rather than serving as God's witness, adding verbal testimony to the witness of the whole creation, Adam took the witness stand against God. Against the witness of the Spirit, the testimony of the whole creation, and even the glory, beauty, and integrity of his own high office, Adam perjured himself."[10] The first sin represented the first step of humanity turning their back on God, who would never turn his back on them. Once that turning took place, humanity oriented toward death. Horton continues, "Instead of being eschatologically oriented toward Sabbath life with God, each other, and the whole creation, we grow increasingly aware that we are [oriented toward death.]"[11] God created us for life, but death tempted us. He provided shalom, and we chose chaos.

## CONCLUSION

Kristin Hannah's novel *Four Winds* tells the story of the Dust Bowl, America's greatest man-made natural disaster, through the life of Elsa Martinelli. It's 1934 in Texas, and Elsa has a choice to make. She can either stay in Texas and try to save her land or take her

---

10. Horton, *Christian Faith*, 410–11.
11. Horton, *Christian Faith*, 413.

family West to California with hopes that she can find a better life for her kids. She opts for the latter. After many dirt-covered, exhausting days and weeks of travel while still hopeful, she is confronted by the reality of death. The work and wages promised were nonexistent. Resources were short, and the landowners knew it. They promised one amount, but they dropped the wage to mere pennies if they got too many workers. Whenever Elsa got work, she had to leave her children behind in the makeshift refugee camp they had come to call home. Fierce competition in the camps led to fights for resources and work.

Man's craving for more led to the Dust Bowl that raged for years, causing families like Elsa's to lose everything. But every so often in this tale of despair, life glimmers, like in Elsa's relationship with her daughter, Loreda. In a moment of hopelessness, Elsa encourages her daughter, "You are of me, Loreda, in a way that can never be broken. Not by words or anger or actions or time. I love you. I will always love you."[12] Life springs forth in the presence of death, even in the lives of humanity after the fall. Because as Loreda was to Elsa, so we are to God. We are of God, and nothing can stop him from loving us, not even death.

Death is our greatest enemy because it is all-encompassing. It's not just about biological death but about the breaking of shalom. God gave humanity relationships to help them thrive, but sin fractured them. Instead of resting in God's love, we fear his rejection and wrath. Instead of trusting one another, we compete with and view each other as threats. Instead of cultivating and caring for the earth, we toil with it, use it, and often abuse it. Not only are we confronted with death when we stand next to a casket, but we are confronted with death whenever we see the brokenness of our relationship with God, others, and creation. Yet, God does not give up on us. Instead, he does whatever it takes to bring us back into shalom, even by entering the chaos of death himself.

---

12. Hannah, *Four Winds*, 310.

# 3

## Saved Through Death

*For if, by the trespass of the one man, death reigned through that one man, how much more will those who receive God's abundant provision of grace and of the gift of righteousness reign in life through the one man, Jesus Christ!*

ROMANS 5:17

*The death of the Lord our God should not be a cause of shame for us; rather, it should be our greatest hope, our greatest glory. In taking upon himself the death that he found in us, he has most faithfully promised to give us life in him, such as we cannot have of ourselves.*

AUGUSTINE

IN ANTHONY DOERR'S NOVEL *Cloud Cuckoo Land*, Konstance lives on the *Argos*, a space shuttle filled with a remnant of humankind flying through space toward a distant planet. On Konstance's twelfth birthday, the present is an invitation into the library, a virtual reality through which she can access every book, movie, or painting humanity has ever made. It's a digital collection of humankind's history. Within the library is Atlas, an immersive map that the *Argos*'s passengers can use to explore Earth as it was before *Argos* launched. Imagine Google Maps street view. Mrs. Flowers, one of the *Argos*'s elders, shows Konstance Atlas before anything else in the library. While in Atlas, Mrs. Flowers shares more with Konstance about the nature of their flight and their goal. Interestingly, she describes a battle against the great enemy of death. "For as long as we have been a species, we humans have tried to defeat death. None of us ever has."[1] Konstance recalls Mrs. Flowers's words after a virus breaks out on the shuttle, and her father tries comforting her with the words, "On Earth, when I was a boy, most everybody got sick. Rashes, funny little fevers. . . . It's part of being human."[2]

The fight to defeat death continues. Countless scientists, doctors, and engineers work together to develop new vaccines, medications, and technologies that prevent illness, defend against viruses, and extend the average lifespan. Yuval Harari's reflection on our history as a species pointedly concludes,

> Until recently, you would not have heard scientists, or anyone else, speak so bluntly. "Defeat death?! What nonsense! We are only trying to cure cancer, tuberculosis, and Alzheimer's disease," they insisted. People avoided the issue of death because the goal seemed too elusive. Why create unreasonable expectations? We're now at a point, however, where we can be frank about it. The leading project of the Scientific Revolution is to give humankind eternal life.[3]

A decade has already passed since Harari published this bold claim. According to research, there were about 55.22 million deaths in 2014, but as a result of the COVID-19 pandemic, that number jumped to 69.25 million deaths in 2021.[4] Our goal may be eternal life, but we are coming up short time and again.

1. Doerr, *Cloud Cuckoo Land*, 212–13.
2. Doer, *Cloud Cuckoo Land*, 267.
3. Harari, *Sapiens*, 35.
4. Our World in Data, "Deaths per Year."

## A HOPEFUL DEATH

Yet, in a spirit of celebration and hope, Christians proclaim, "Christ has died." What we are trying to defeat, that scares us most, is what we hold at our very core. We wear necklaces with first-century torture devices hanging from them. We sing hymns like "Lift High the Cross" or "When I Survey the Wondrous Cross," which exalt the demise of Jesus Christ on the cross. We make the sign of the cross after we pray. We remember Christ's death as we partake in the bread and wine. Christians are rather odd on this account.

Glorifying a first-century Jewish man's death may be strange to many, but for Christians, the death of Christ is the greatest hope for defeating death. The apostle Paul wrote, "Just as one trespass resulted in condemnation for all people, so also one righteous act resulted in justification and life for all people."[5] Adam's sin opened shalom's door to death, but Jesus' death kicked death out of shalom's house forever. Jesus' death was the one righteous act that overcame the one trespass of Adam. As one of my first theology professors, John Clark, was fond of saying in class, "Just as Satan was about to pierce Jesus' heart with his sword, Jesus turned around and slew Satan." With only the power of his death, Jesus defeated the enemy.

## THE TRANSFORMATION OF DEATH

But why death? Wasn't there another way? To many people, the death of Jesus Christ appears barbaric. Take Charlie, for example. He has a tough exterior and can come across as distant, but over time we've built enough trust to speak candidly about religion, politics, and many other topics. He's not a Christian but has been around Christians enough to understand much of what we believe. Sometimes, I've shared with him titles of hymns and Scripture passages that I'm using to lead worship services. One time, he was struck by how often the word "blood" came up in Christian hymns. He mocked it by saying, "How much blood do we need?" He didn't like the idea of God killing his Son. He especially didn't

---

5. Rom 5:18.

like the idea that God's Son died because of the sins he, Charlie, had committed throughout his life. The gospel is offensive because of Christ's death. Jesus' death makes a scandal out of the gospel. It doesn't sit well with folks like Charlie. Maybe it doesn't sit well with you either. Yet, it's one of many ways that God uses the unexpected to bring about transformation.

After humanity's fall into sin, God immediately transformed death for redemption. God didn't abandon his people when he banished them from the garden; instead, he gave them the grace they needed to continue outside paradise. God clothed Adam and Eve just before he expelled them from Eden. "The LORD God made garments of skin for Adam and his wife and clothed them."[6] These garments of skin were made from dead animals and offered to Adam and Eve as protection against the elements and coverings for the shame they felt from being naked.

Did God kill those animals? Maybe. Or, as John Calvin argues, God taught humans to kill so that they might live. Calvin writes,

> It is not indeed proper to understand his words, as if God had been a furrier, or a servant to sew clothes. No, it is not credible that skins should have been presented to them by chance; but, since animals had before been destined for their use, being now impelled by a new necessity, they put some to death, in order to cover themselves with their skins, having been divinely directed to adopt this counsel; therefore Moses calls God the Author of it.[7]

If Calvin is correct, then God worked through people to put to death the animals that would serve as their covering and sustenance. He prepared them for life in the wild.

Instead of thinking of death only as the penalty for sin, God's grace makes it possible for Adam and Eve to see death as a doorway to life. With animal skins, they could keep themselves and their children warm and protected and, at the same time, be able to cook a hearty stew. They could pass on this knowledge to the next

---

6. Gen 3:21.
7. Calvin, *Genesis*, 181.

generation so that they too might care for their children and their aging parents. God's free gift of grace through death traces back to these moments before and after the garden of Eden was closed.

Death is also redemptive in the story of Israel. Take the Passover, for example. Passover revolved around the death of a lamb, and through that death, Israel was saved. Moses called on Pharaoh to let his people go, but time and again, Pharaoh refused. After several plagues that destroyed the Egyptian way of life, Moses said to Pharaoh, "Every firstborn son in Egypt will die, from the firstborn son of Pharaoh, who sits on the throne, to the firstborn son of the female slave, who is at her hand mill, and all the firstborn of the cattle as well."[8] God commanded his people to take a lamb large enough to feed each of their families and spread its blood on the doorposts of the home where they ate. If there were not enough members in a family to eat all of the lamb, they shared the leftovers with their neighbors. As a result, death passed over their homes, and their firstborn children lived. Death ravaged Egypt, but God spared his people through the death of a lamb.

The Passover was both a sacrifice and a sacrament. It was a sacrifice because the people killed the lamb and used the blood as a sign that spared their lives. Yet, it was also a sacrament because the lamb became a meal for the people to commune with God and one another. Through one lamb's death, God reconnected humanity to one another and with him. As the theologian Herman Bavinck writes, "The significance of these meals was that God met with his people and, on the basis of the sacrifice made and accepted, united himself with his people in joy."[9] Since God accepted the sacrifice of the Passover, he communed with his people through the meal and preserved their lives. God's shalom continued to break into the chaos of death.

---

8. Exod 11:5.
9. Bavinck, *Holy Spirit*, 541–42.

## THE TRANSFORMATIVE DEATH OF CHRIST

In the New Testament, we read of another sacrifice and sacrament, and that sacrifice is the death of Jesus Christ, the perfect lamb of God. Like the lamb at Passover, Jesus' shed blood is a sign to God that he will spare his people from judgment. Unlike the lamb at Passover, Jesus is the sacrificial lamb, and he is the God to whom he presents the sacrifice. Therefore, Jesus permanently satisfies God's requirements for sacrifice and thus puts an end to the need for further blood offerings.

Through Jesus' sacrificial death, we are made one with God. The shed blood of Christ cleanses humanity and provides a way through death and back into a relationship with God. Theologians call this the doctrine of atonement. Various theories explain how atonement works, but the key idea in atonement is that God and humanity are brought back together in a union.

Jesus Christ embodies this atonement within himself. He bridges the divide between heaven and earth in his own body. In John 2, Jesus enters the Jewish temple and begins flipping tables and running people and animals out of the temple courts. At first, it seems like an odd moment in Jesus' life, but seen through the lens of God's mission to restore relationships—with him, one another, and creation—it takes on deeper meaning. The people in the temple courts had cheapened the sacrificial systems. By selling animals on site, they were making it convenient for God's people to show up and offer a sacrifice to God. Although convenient, temple merchants took away the heart of what the sacrifice was all about. The sacrifice was about connecting with God through prayer and worship, not just checking another box on one's to-do list. As always, God doesn't just want his people to go through the motions; he wants their hearts. After Jesus cleansed the temple, the Jews asked him, "'What sign can you show us to prove your authority to do all this?' Jesus answered them, 'Destroy this temple, and I will raise it again in three days.'"[10] Flabbergasted, the Jews can't believe that Jesus can rebuild the temple in three days when

---

10. John 2:18–19.

it had taken them more than four decades to build it themselves. Of course, Jesus wasn't talking about the building; he was talking about his body. He had the authority to determine what happened in the temple because he was the truer and better temple. Just as the Jews came to the temple to meet God, and it was in the temple that God chose to meet them, so in Jesus' body, humanity and God met. Wherever Jesus is, there is the temple of God. As a result, in the New Testament, the church is called God's temple. The Holy Spirit makes a home in our body, and we no longer have to go to some place to meet God; instead, he meets us in our own bodies.[11]

So, how does this talk about the temple relate to atonement? Jesus, the true temple, not only embodied the meeting place but also took on the role of the priest offering the sacrifice and that of the sacrifice itself. Jesus' death exemplifies how costly, inconvenient, and radical God's call on our life is and what is required to bring us back into union with God. God knows we cannot come to him with true devotion, so through Jesus, he took on our humanity, lived out perfect faith, and bore our punishment in his death.

What's more, Jesus' death becomes a sacrament as he names his body and blood in the meal of bread and wine.[12] Like the Passover lamb, the sacrifice of Jesus not only saves us from judgment but connects us with God and one another. Rowan Williams, an Anglican bishop, comments,

> As Jesus meets with his friends for that last supper and tells them to see the broken Bread and Wine poured out as his body and blood which are about to be broken and poured out in crucifixion, he says in effect, "what is going to happen to me, the suffering and death I'm about to endure, the tearing of my flesh and the shedding of my blood, is to be the final, the definitive, sign of God's welcome and God's mercy." Instead of being the ultimate tragedy and disaster, it is an open door into the welcome of the Father.[13]

11. 1 Cor 6:19.
12. Matt 26:26–30.
13. Williams, *Being Christian*, 47.

Through Jesus' death, we experience his full embrace, and through the bread and wine, we remember that his door is never closed to us.

Yet, remembering Christ's death is not just an intellectual exercise but a spiritual uniting with Jesus Christ. His death meets us in the here and now of our lives. "We always carry around in our body the death of Jesus, so that the life of Jesus may also be revealed in our body."[14] We want the resurrected life of Jesus, but that only comes through his death. Anthony Thiselton writes,

> To remember God's mighty acts . . . is not simply to call them to mind but to assign to them an active role within one's "world." "To remember" God is to engage in worship, trust, and obedience, just as "to forget" God is to turn one's back on him. Failure to remember is not absent-mindedness but unfaithfulness to the covenant and disobedience. "Remembering" the gospel tradition . . . transforms attitude and action.[15]

By remembering Jesus' death, we are reconnected to the life source that was once ours in the garden. As the life source of God renews us, we will be transformed holistically and over time.

There are still those who argue that when Jesus said to "remember" his death, Christians are to do so in a memorial way. This approach to the Lord's Supper originates in the Protestant Reformation through the works of Swiss reformer Ulrich Zwingli, whose followers can be found today in many Anabaptist churches in the West, but has influenced broader Evangelicalism in America as well. To those who say the Lord's Supper is only a memorial or an intellectual exercise, Herman Bavinck replies that there is more on the table than we think. "It is not merely a reminiscence of or a reflection on Christ's benefits but a most intimate bonding with Christ himself, just as food and drink are united with our body."[16] Through the Lord's Supper, we are intimately united all the more with Jesus Christ. A spiritual union takes place within the renewal

---

14. 2 Cor 4:10.
15. Thiselton, *Corinthians*, 879.
16. Bavinck, *Holy Spirit*, 567.

of remembering. Our suffering becomes his suffering, and his suffering becomes ours. Our death is his death, and his death is our death. John Calvin said,

> First, we must understand that as long as Christ remains outside of us, and we are separated from him, all that he has suffered and done for the salvation of the human race remains useless and of no value to us. Therefore, to share in what he has received from the Father, he has to become ours and to dwell within us. . . . For, as I have said, all that he possesses is nothing to us until we grow into one body with him.[17]

This remembrance at the table is a profoundly spiritual and material event. The sacrament changes us and makes us more like Christ because the Holy Spirit gives it to us as a means of grace.

## THE COMFORT OF THE CROSS

Through Jesus Christ's death, we also find solace in our suffering. As Jesus clothed himself with a robe of flesh, he invited all the facets of human pain, stress, and heartache into his life. He no longer knew the security of the Father's right hand. Instead, he knew the small space of Mary's womb, the cool night air on his soft infant skin, and the hunger pangs that come so often to a baby. He knew the growing pains of puberty, the pain of a scraped knee, and the grief of death in one's community. He knew what it felt like to be rejected, misunderstood, and overlooked. He suffered in every way humans do but at no time more acutely than in his death. Even before he was in custody, he anticipated the misery of his death. He said to his disciples in John 12:27, "Now my soul is troubled, and what shall I say? 'Father, save me from this hour'? No, it was for this very reason I came to this hour." His disciples' greatest wish was that Jesus would not suffer. Yet, despite the anxiety and dread Jesus may have felt, he committed to surrendering his life to death

---

17. Calvin, *Institutes*, 3.1.1.

because it was the only hope for ever uniting heaven and earth again.

He was spared no pain despite his fortitude and commitment to his mission. We see this magnified as he cried out from the cross, "My God, my God, why have you forsaken me?"[18] In these words, the cry of every person who has felt the scourge of injustice is heard, from Abel's blood crying out from the dirt to the cry of the martyrs in Rev 6. In this moment of abandonment, Jesus suffers in solidarity with every human being who has ever gone through some kind of hell on earth.

By going through hell, Jesus' death also delivers justice to the oppressed. God must bring the unjust actions of men and women through the ages to justice. We all feel this whenever we read news of a mass shooting, terrorist bombing, or serial killer. We demand that the innocent see justice and the perpetrator be punished. We feel the need for justice when we see a black man in police custody killed, homeless people filling the streets while a few live in multimillion dollar homes, and melting ice caps affecting many of the world's poorest regions before those with power make lasting change. Our world needs judgment because sin has made a mockery of God's good creation. Yet, no matter how many years someone sits in prison, the lost loved one doesn't come back. No matter how many corrupt police officers get convicted, jail time won't undo decades of police brutality. True judgment comes when the great enemy of humanity, sin and the devil, is put to death. That's why Jesus delivered justice through his death. In his death, he not only carried the weight of all our sins but also the judgment of all the injustices perpetrated everywhere throughout history. He bore the punishment that the vilest of people deserved because only he had the power to hold that injustice, take it to death, and raise up the loved ones we long to see. God promises justice through Jesus Christ, and his justice truly brings about the lasting change for which we long.

By sinning against our Creator, every one of us became his enemies. The apostle Paul makes our position before God abundantly

---

18. Matt 27:46.

clear, "All have sinned and fallen short of the glory of God."[19] All who live commit injustices. Of course, it does seem like some of us are far more heinous than others, but we've all tasted sweet revenge. We've all lashed out in ways that have hurt the innocent. We are all part of systems that oppress people experiencing poverty. Injustice is so prevalent, like we're stuck in a hundred-foot-deep pit, we just can't escape it.

## CONCLUSION

Jesus proved his unconditional love for humanity by delivering justice through his death. "Love your enemies" was more than what he preached; it's what he did. The prophet Isaiah says, "We all, like sheep, have gone astray; each of us have turned to our own way." So, Isaiah continues, "the LORD has laid on him the iniquity of us all."[20] Jesus' death brought a once for all pardon for sin. "While we were still sinners, Christ died for us."[21] Jesus' love is so vast that he dies not for the just but for the unjust. For as he said, "It's not the healthy who need a doctor, but the sick."[22] We may never know just how deep sin has penetrated our hearts, but we can rest assured knowing that Jesus Christ loves us enough to die so that he transforms death into a reunion with God.

In God's counterintuitive way, he used Jesus' death as a doorway to life. It seems odd, right? Jesus' death reminds me of Maria Àngels Anglada's novel *The Violin of Auschwitz*. A violin maker named Daniel is imprisoned in Auschwitz during the height of World War II. When the commanding officer of the camp, an avid musical instrument collector, finds out about Daniel, he demands that Daniel craft a violin for him just as elegant as any Stradivarius. So, Daniel spends weeks and months pouring over every last detail of the violin, afraid that if he gets one minute detail wrong, he will

19. Rom 3:23.
20. Isa 53:6.
21. Rom 5:8.
22. Luke 5:31.

be killed or worse, but one day the thought occurs to him, "The whole idea of his violin seemed absurd, like a rose in a pigsty. A violin in the Three Rivers Camp. A violin as a survival tactic."[23] Amid the anxiety of producing the violin, Daniel couldn't help but see the irony in it. Auschwitz was no place for a finely crafted violin, yet the magic of art and music invaded the camp. And just as Auschwitz was no place for such a beautiful instrument, the cross was no place for the prince of heaven to be battered and beaten and put to death, yet there he was; the darkness couldn't hold back the light.

---

23. Anglada, *Violin of Auschwitz*, 48.

# PART 2: CHRIST IS RISEN

# 4

# Death Is Defeated

*Where, O death, is your victory? Where, O death, is your sting?*

1 CORINTHIANS 15:55

*God's script for our drama does not originate from within, but in the history of Jesus Christ—his life, death, and resurrection. That is our history, as ones who belong to Christ.*

J. TODD BILLINGS, *REMEMBRANCE, COMMUNION, AND HOPE*

DEATH HAUNTED THE RUSSIAN novelist Fyodor Dostoevsky. His mother died of tuberculosis when he was just fifteen years old.[1] Two years later, a stroke killed his father. The trauma of his father's death may have even instigated his battle with epilepsy. In the wake of his grief and pain, Dostoevsky turned to reading and writing for solace. Yet, even this practice of comfort brought him face to face with the threat of death. After writing his first novel, *Poor Folk*, in 1845, the literary circles of Saint Petersburg welcomed him in. In 1846, he joined the Petrashevsky Circle, a scholarly group that

---

1. Biographical information draws from Pevear, introduction to *Notes from a Dead House*.

focused on issues related to social reforms in Russia. Although this group claimed to be anti-revolutionary, some members, including Dostoevsky, were working toward political revolution. Eventually, the authorities arrested and sentenced Dostoevsky to death in 1849. However, just before the the firing squad were sent to execute him, an official changed his sentence and instead sent him to a hard labor prison camp in Siberia for four years.

He recounts his prison experiences in his novel *Notes from a Dead House*. From the mundanity of the work assignments and the taste of the prison food to the complicated relationships among inmates serving time for various crimes, Dostoevsky describes the prison experience in excruciating detail from first-person perspective of an inmate. On his release date, as the guards loosen his shackles and the other inmates cheer him on, he thinks to himself,

> The fetters fell off. I picked them up. . . . I wanted to hold them in my hand, to look them over for the last time. It was as if I marveled now that they had just been on my legs. "Well, go with God, go with God!" the prisoners said, their voices abrupt, coarse, but as if pleased at something. Yes, with God! Freedom, a new life, resurrection from the dead.[2]

Upon his release from prison, after a life stalked by death, Dostoevsky experienced something so powerful that he could only describe it as resurrection.

Resurrection is the defeat of death. It is the great reversal, the unexpected, and the surprising. It's what Christians confess when they declare on Easter Sunday, "Christ is risen. He is risen indeed." The resurrection of Jesus Christ is the fulfillment of what God said to the serpent in the garden, "He will crush your head, and you will strike his heel."[3] Fleming Rutledge puts it deftly: "The dominion of Death is blown to bits on Easter Day."[4] Satan struck Jesus' heel by taking him to the grave, but Jesus crushed Satan by defeating death itself.

2. Dostoevsky, *Notes*, 37.
3. Gen 3:15.
4. Rutledge, *Means of Grace*, 129–30.

We all long for resurrection amid a world full of death. We want the fear of school shootings, cancer, and dementia to be vanquished forever. We want to grow old with the confidence that whatever suffering may come, it will only be temporary. Jesus' resurrection guarantees Christians that death has been defeated. We no longer need to be controlled by fear but can be empowered by resurrection joy and courage.

## RESURRECTION JOY

The early church experienced joy amid suffering firsthand. Jesus' disciple, Peter, encouraged these churches, writing,

> In his great mercy he has given us new birth into a living hope through the resurrection of Jesus Christ from the dead, and into an inheritance that can never perish, spoil or fade. This inheritance is kept in heaven for you, who through faith are shielded by God's power until the coming of the salvation that is ready to be revealed in the last time. In all this you greatly rejoice, though now for a little while you may have had to suffer grief in all kinds of trials.[5]

The Christian's hope is a living hope found in the resurrected body of Jesus Christ. Jesus will never perish, spoil, or fade; he is secure in heaven, waiting for the day when he will make all things new. Therefore, we rejoice because we are held fast in this hope.

Peter wrote these words in the context of political dictatorship. Emperor Nero saw Christians as a direct threat to his rule.[6] If they were not worshiping him like his other loyal subjects, then he thought they must be revolutionists. So, like any power-hungry narcissist, he responded with violence. Therefore, as Peter penned this letter, he wrote with the awareness that Nero's henchmen had already murdered some of his friends and neighbors and his name was not far down the list. He knew his number would be up soon,

---

5. 1 Pet 1:3–6.
6. Overview of Nero and the early Christians draws from McKnight, *1 Peter*, 29.

and he would not have the luxury of writing letters to his parishioners for much longer. He wrote with a Spirit-filled fury. He needed to communicate every inch of the resurrected Christ to his people. His life might be near its end, but the Christians who would receive his letter needed the wings of resurrection to persevere in joy amid persecution.

Peter's congregations received his letter as exiles. Due to Nero's anti-Christian policies, they had to run for their lives. They no longer had the haven of their Jewish communities. They were now living on the fringe of society. People accused them of being a part of a cult that ate the flesh and drank the blood of their crucified God. They had zero political power. They had no rights. They did everything they could just to survive. They did not have a church building with beautiful stained glass to call their own. They worshiped in their temporary homes while under the threat of death. They lived by faith and not by sight.

There are still many Christians around the world today who live under the threat of pain and death, but most of us in the West find it difficult to relate to this kind of anxiety amid worship. We are free to attend any church in our communities on Sundays. We enjoy fellowship over church potlucks and Bible studies. We sing "Christ the Lord Is Risen Today!" every Easter, but we don't spend much time thinking about our mortality, let alone the possibility that some Christians are murdered for their belief in Jesus. Yet, Peter's words of resurrection joy can still speak into our lives today. Suffering plagues everyone regardless of geographical location, wealth, poverty, or faith. As the ethicist and theologian Lewis Smedes wrote, "To qualify as sufferers, we must want to be rid of something with such passion that it hurts. Suffering is having to endure what we very much want not to endure."[7] This means that breaking free from an addiction, the seemingly permanent gray clouds of depression, or the heart-wrenching grief that won't stop nagging are all forms of suffering during which, Peter believes, we can experience resurrection joy. It's an audacious claim, but if it's true, it's the best news we can hear in seasons of suffering.

7. Smedes, *Love Within Limits*, 1.

## Death Is Defeated

At first, it might seem odd to imagine how one man's resurrection from the dead could bring joy to his followers years later, but the source of joy that the living Jesus provides comes from his resolute commitment to human beings and the rest of creation. Jesus refuses to abandon us to the grave. He is the word that spoke the world into existence. He called creation "good"! He will not let suffering, sickness, and death destroy the joy of life. N. T. Wright puts it succinctly, "The message of the resurrection is that this world matters!"[8] If this world matters to God, then our trials are not the final chapter. No, suffering will not have the final say. Death will not win. The resurrection of Jesus Christ assures his people that we can live with joy. Dare I say we can laugh in the face of suffering because Jesus is alive? As Peter puts it, "Though you have not seen him, you love him; and even though you do not see him now, you believe in him and are filled with an *inexpressible and glorious joy*, for you are receiving the end result of your faith, *the salvation of your souls.*"[9] Because we are secure in Jesus Christ, we can know glorious joy in the face of adversity!

Does that mean Christians are immune to sorrow? No! Does that mean Christians should learn to ignore their sorrow to focus on joy? No! Because Jesus lowered himself into the depths of suffering like a mountaineer lowered into a crevasse, we are set free from the fear of our pain. Through Christ's resurrection, God empowers us to face our pain head-on because he assures us our pain will not have the final say. The joy of being secure in Christ allows us to be present while suffering. "You don't run from sorrow. You don't have to. The joy enables you to just have sorrow."[10] We don't need to numb it out with alcohol or television. Instead, we can descend into the depths with Jesus as our guide, knowing he will not abandon us to the grave. Jesus knows how brutal suffering is and how tempting it is to want to escape it, but he promises he will guide us through suffering to resurrection.

8. Wright, *For All God's Worth*, 65.
9. 1 Pet 1:8–9, emphasis added.
10. Keller, "Born into Hope."

As a young boy, every Sunday at nine fifteen in the morning, I sat in a small room across the table from Mr. Stamos. Shoulder to shoulder with five or six other boys in the second grade Sunday school class, we loved listening to Mr. Stamos's lessons. He was a lifelong science teacher. He loved talking to us as much as he enjoyed teaching us. He was never too formal or casual with us to ignore our questions or not take them seriously. He listened intently and answered honestly. He always seemed ready for a belly laugh. His contagious laughter created a learning environment where I felt God was okay with us laughing, too. I distinctly remember his storytelling. He loved telling us about when a stray dog jumped in front of his bike while delivering newspapers as a boy. This captivated us. Mr. Stamos knew his audience.

We'd hear the bell ringing down the hallway when the Sunday school hour ended. It wasn't like a bell at school. It was a bronze handbell, always Rick the Ringer. I don't know how Rick got the bell ringer job, but he rang faithfully week after week. Rick was a balding middle-aged man with Down syndrome who sported a graying mustache and exuded more joy than most adults at church. His happiness seemed odd because of his diagnosis. My second grade assumption was that if a child were born with a disability, then he would be more depressed than people without a disability. Yet, the opposite was true for Rick. He seemed in touch with a level of joy that most people never experience.

Both Mr. Stamos and Rick exemplified Christian joy. Neither achieved greatness according to the world's standards, but they knew deep and abiding joy. As followers of the resurrected Lord, we, too, can experience deep joy amid everyday experiences. Christian joy does not depend on circumstances, good looks, or an adrenaline rush. Someone with an extra chromosome or many years behind them can find lasting joy. Joy is dependent upon something far more significant than our circumstances. Joy finds its source in the resurrection of Jesus Christ.

## RESURRECTION COURAGE

Remaining present in our suffering will require us to be courageous. Like joy, our courage doesn't come from who we are but who Jesus is. He is the courageous One who obeyed God, even unto death. He was obedient because a fear of pain did not control him. A fear of God controlled him. As Christians, we are God-fearing people. When we allow our fear to be in its proper place, we will have all the courage to face our pain.

Isabel Allende's novel *The Long Petal of the Sea* begins with a war in Spain. The main character, Victor Dalmau, completed three years of medical school before joining the war effort as a medic. He was not an official doctor, but the war required him to go above and beyond what usually would have been expected of a medic. One day a young boy, not older than sixteen, showed up in the camp on a stretcher. There was no telling how long he had been lying wounded on the battlefield, but it was obvious to everyone that there was nothing they could do for the young man. In a last-ditch effort, Victor unwrapped the bandage on the boy's chest. To his surprise, the wound was perfectly clean and yet wide open. He could see the heart beating slower and slower until it finally stopped. The boy gave one last exhale and died. Then, to everyone's surprise, including his own, Victor "inserted three fingers of his right hand into the gaping wound, gently grasped the organ, and squeezed it rhythmically several times, quite calmly and naturally, for how long, he couldn't remember: perhaps thirty seconds, or perhaps an eternity. Suddenly, he felt the heart coming back to life between his fingers, first with an almost imperceptible tremor, soon with a strong, regular beat." Victor had no right to make such a daring medical decision, but as he said to a nearby doctor, "I thought there was nothing to lose."[11] In other words, the fear of making a mistake could have overwhelmed Victor, but his fear of doing nothing drove him to act courageously.

Our fear of God invites us into a life of courage in the Christian life. Like Victor, when we fear the right thing, we will be

---

11. Allende, *Long Petal*, 5.

willing to live courageously. That right thing isn't a thing at all. It's a person. We must fear God. When we fear God, our other fears will diminish, and the courage to face the most demanding circumstances in life will grow within us. Peter encourages his churches to fear God rather than their circumstances:

> Since you call on a Father who judges each person's work impartially, live out your time as foreigners here *in reverent fear*. For you know that it was not with perishable things such as silver or gold that you were redeemed from the empty way of life handed down to you from your ancestors, *but with the precious blood of Christ*, a lamb without blemish or defect. He was chosen before the creation of the world, but was revealed in these last times for your sake. Through him *you believe in God*, who raised him from the dead and glorified him, and so *your faith and hope are in God*.[12]

Peter proclaims reverent fear of God because God is powerful enough to raise the dead and loving enough to sacrifice his own Son for us. Therefore, whatever circumstances we face, even if they are fatal, need not control us because we know the One who is more powerful than death itself. To summarize Viktor E. Frankl's *Man's Search for Meaning*, life only has meaning if we have hope that even suffering and death cannot destroy. God promises that in Jesus, we, too, will be raised because he has committed himself to us in love through the blood of his Son. Therefore, we need not fear anyone or anything other than God himself.

The story of David and Goliath is a classic example of fearing God more than one's circumstances in Scripture. Young David is a model of how to face fear when God is on your side.

In 1 Sam 17, David is carrying a YETI cooler full of sandwiches and Monster Energy drinks to his three oldest brothers in the valley of Elah. They are camped out with the rest of their army buddies, waiting to go to war with the Philistines. In those days, there were no cargo planes or helicopters to make supply drops, so family members relied on each other for food and drink. As David

---

12. 1 Pet 1:17–21, emphasis added.

walks up to camp, he hears some yelling. He can't quite make it out over the hustle and bustle of the camp, but it's clear that this voice has struck terror in the soldiers. He begins asking around and finds out that the Philistines have challenged Israel to a one-man war: an ancient war tactic that prevents further bloodshed by offering one man to fight another, and the winner takes all. In this case, whoever won enslaved their enemies. The voice David kept hearing was the Philistines' warrior named Goliath. Everyone kept telling David how big he was, but he had to see it to believe. This guy was massive. I'm talking at least six feet nine and three hundred pounds of muscle. No wonder everyone was afraid. Yet, David didn't let his fear of man overpower his fear of God.

Perspective often changes everything. When the Israelites saw Goliath, they kept saying to each other, "He comes out to defy Israel."[13] Whereas, when David saw Goliath, he said, "Who is this uncircumcised Philistine that he should defy the armies of the living God?"[14] Notice the contrasting responses. The Israelites were focused on Goliath's disrespect for them, while David saw through to the heart of the issue. Goliath wasn't just disrespecting Israel; he was disrespecting the living God—the God whom David had been anointed by to be the next king of Israel. David knew the stories of this God: the water turned to blood, the millions of locusts, the death of the firstborn in Egypt, the dividing of the Red Sea, the water from the rock, and the manna from heaven. David knew this God was mightier than any man, no matter how much this Philistine could bench press.

So, freed from fear of man by his fear of God, David could think creatively about approaching Goliath. Instead of wearing King Saul's armor and sword to fight him sword to sword, he picks up five smooth stones and a sling. David wasn't interested in playing by the war standards of the day. He was acting subversively in the name of God. Malcolm Gladwell explains,

---

13. 1 Sam 17:25.
14. 1 Sam 17:26.

Paintings from medieval times show slingers hitting birds in midflight. Irish slingers were said to be able to hit a coin from as far away as they could see it, and in the Old Testament Book of Judges, slingers are described as being accurate within a "hair's breadth." An experienced slinger could kill or seriously injure a target at a distance of up to two hundred yards.[15]

David, who had slain lions and bears with his sling, chose to face Goliath with the same tactic. In other words, David brought a gun to a sword fight, and Goliath didn't stand a chance.

David's fear of God versus the Israelites' fear of Goliath were two different kinds of fear. Fear of Goliath fanned terror's flame. Fear of God nurtured assured confidence. The New Testament scholar Scot McKnight comments on this difference of fears. He says, "This fear [of God] is neither dread nor anxiety; rather, it is the healthy response of a human being before an altogether different kind of being, God, and is a sign of spiritual health and gratitude. This holy Judge we now call 'Father,' a term indicating intimacy and love but also respect and submission."[16] When we are in a right relationship with God, we fear him rather than the world, and we find that he transforms our fear into the intimate love that he has always wanted from us.

Matt and Hannah were examples of David in my life. We met when I was still in college. They had recently graduated and married. Matt was in graduate school for theology, and Hannah was studying social work. Both would eventually go on to complete PhDs in theology. When deciding where to rent an apartment, I asked Matt for advice. He and Hannah lived in the Austin neighborhood in Chicago's West Side. At the time, Austin was Chicago's poorest and most violent neighborhood. Strangely, this successful couple had chosen to live in such a tough neighborhood. Why would they put themselves at risk to live in a community that lacked the amenities most white millennials were looking for? It turns out that during college, Matt read N. T. Wright's book

---

15. Gladwell, *David and Goliath*, 9.
16. McKnight, *1 Peter*, 89.

*Simply Christian*, and he had a come-to-Jesus moment about how he should live his life. He learned that following Jesus' way meant walking a path of downward mobility. Turns out, people don't find life's most significant meaning in getting the next job promotion, buying a bigger house, or being in the best school district. True meaning comes from following Jesus to the cross, dying to the self, and experiencing resurrection. Matt and Hannah modeled this by living in an overlooked and often discarded neighborhood. Most people I knew then were terrified of even going for a walk in the Austin neighborhood, but Matt and Hannah didn't follow that narrative. They lived, walked, and found deep friendships in Austin. They became known as that "white couple" on the block. They learned to suffer with their neighbors, march in protests for Black Lives Matter, and be present where God had led them. Like David, fear did not control them. Instead, they lived with a secure knowledge that the God they served was greater than anything a "dangerous" neighborhood could throw at them.

When we fear God more than anything else, we find where our true hope lies. Hope doesn't lie in the things that can pass away, like money, possessions, and status. We can't find ultimate hope in people who can choose to walk away and abandon us. We can only find true hope in the God who has bound himself to us through the blood of his Son and has shown us that blood leads to resurrection. The God we fear is one who never quits and is never defeated. As Tim Keller once said, "There's no way to get through life unless you know how to get through suffering and there's no way to get through suffering unless you have a living hope."[17] Jesus is our living hope. He will guide us through suffering because he has died and risen again.

The great defeat of death in Jesus Christ's resurrection transforms Christians from people of gloom and fear to people of joy and courage. The solid rock of Jesus Christ is the foundation on which we build our lives. Like Dostoevsky's prisoner, we can start every day feeling like the fetters have fallen off and we are experiencing resurrection. Like young David, we can confess that every

---

17. Keller, "Born into Hope."

assault on God's people is actually an assault on him. Like Matt and Hannah, we can trust that the God of resurrection is a God who is with us no matter where we go.

# 5

# Life Is Secure

*I give them eternal life, and they shall never perish; no one will snatch them out of my hand. My Father, who has given them to me, is greater than all; no one can snatch them out of my Father's hand.*

JOHN 10:28–29

*Q. What is your only comfort
in life and in death?*

*A. That I am not my own,
but belong—
body and soul,
in life and in death—
to my faithful Savior, Jesus Christ.*

HEIDELBERG CATECHISM Q&A 1

COMPANIES MARKET SECURITY PRODUCTS to Americans daily. If we buy these products, we will be able to secure our future and the future of those we love. These products come in all shapes and sizes: life insurance, retirement portfolios, home security systems, password management software, weight loss strategies, diets, etc. The list can go on and on. We're told, "Buy this thing and you'll sleep well tonight."

We crouch like a catcher waiting for the promised pitch to land in our glove, but security always escapes us. Job loss, divorce, depression, anxiety, death, etc. happen without a moment's notice. All of a sudden, you're left with nothing. When I was eight years old, a tornado ripped through our farm one stormy night, turning evergreen trees on their head and destroying half our barn. That tornado did not ask my permission to damage my family's property. Life is unpredictable. Even when we feel like we are taking all the proper steps to save for retirement, plan for emergencies, and protect our homes and children, we still face circumstances that leave us shaken and insecure.

## DEATH DESTABILIZES LIFE

The most obvious threat to our security is death. It doesn't matter how much money you have, what kind of car you drive, or what college your kid goes to; if death remains a possibility, then life is not fully secure. As of this moment, the death rate for human beings hovers around 100 percent. There is not much hope for avoiding it.

When we are honest and think about our loved ones and friends who have died, we know that it destabilizes our sense of tranquility. In my first year of college, I was enjoying my newfound freedoms, living three hours away from home. I was staying up late, hanging out with friends, and not too concerned about how well I was doing with my studies. Life was good! Then, I got a message on Facebook from a high school friend named Tim. Our mutual friend, Becky, was in a coma. She took too much Tylenol after drinking too much alcohol. Within a week, she was dead. I didn't know how to respond or what to do. I was so shocked that I didn't even set up travel plans to get back home in time for the funeral service. I felt lost, confused, angry, and sad, all at the same time. Life was no longer "good."

During high school, Becky and I worked at the local grocery store together. When we weren't serving customers deli-sliced ham or checking people through at the cash register, she often told stories about her weekend adventures. It never took long for her to draw me into a laughing fit. She wasn't afraid to act the fool and lighten the room's mood. She was the kind of person that was just fun to be around. So, when I found out she was dead at sixteen, I felt unnerved. How could she be gone?

Becky's death became my point of no return. I had to wrestle deeply with the implications of my faith in Jesus Christ. Jesus' resurrection is supposed to make life secure, but everything around me was screaming how insecure life really is. So, I had a choice. I could either pretend everything was fine by stuffing my feelings deep down inside, hoping they would one day go away; I could blame God for failing to protect Becky and abandon my faith; or I could see if my faith could hold up under the weight of my sorrow. The twentieth-century preacher George Buttrick once said in a sermon at the Harvard University chapel, "God is found as we face adverse facts and yet keep faith."[1] We don't find God by running away from him or pretending our sorrow doesn't exist. We see God as we face grief and cry out to him throughout the process. Ultimately, this was true in my experience, and I've seen it happen in other people's lives. God meets us in the suffering.

Jesus' own words give voice to all those who are frustrated by the insecurity of life. As Jesus cried out amid his most sorrowful and painful moment on the cross, "My God, my God, why have you forsaken me?" you hear the voice of a man facing the pain and grief of his most brutal moment on earth in faith. In his voice, we find our quivering voice resonating profoundly within the Divine. Yet, if you read the Gospels' account of Jesus' death, God does not help, fix, or save Jesus from suffering. The insecurity of life wins the day. The power of death even vanquishes the incarnate Son of God.

---

1. Buttrick, *Sermons*, 115.

## BELONGING TO GOD BRINGS SECURITY

However, Jesus' faith continues to shine through his darkest hour. "Father, into your hands I commit my spirit."[2] His only comfort in the face of death was that he was not his own but belonged body and soul to his Father in heaven. That same comfort is ours. As the Heidelberg Catechism puts it, "What is your only comfort in life and in death? That I am not my own, but belong—body and soul, in life and in death—to my faithful Savior, Jesus Christ."[3] If Jesus died and did not rise, then the comfort of belonging to him would be null and void. But since he lives just three days after his death, we know that life is more secure than we ever expected.

If the comfort God gave to Jesus on the cross is available to us all, why do we find ourselves resisting him? Why is it so hard to accept that we are not our own, but belong to God? Why do we so desperately hold on to the view that we belong to ourselves? Alan Noble wrote an entire book on this question and he concluded, "If we are our own, we need to justify everything we do. We need to know that we are optimizing and competing and improving. But if we are not our own but belong to Christ, things can just be good. And that's enough."[4] If we belong to Christ, then we can go outside and enjoy the beauty of creation without the pressure of needing to use it to benefit our status, careers, or self-fulfillment.

Imagine Sarah. Sarah grew up in a middle-class neighborhood, her parents were both college educated, and she was the youngest of three siblings. Her earliest memories at school were doing projects about what she wanted to be when she grew up: one year it was a teacher because she loved her teacher, the next it was a dancer because she had started tap lessons over the summer, and the next it was mayor because the town mayor had visited her school. Her teachers and her parents kept encouraging her, year after year, that she could be anyone or do anything she put her mind to. If she believed in herself enough, then nothing was impossible.

---

2. Luke 23:46.
3. Christian Reformed Church, "Heidelberg Catechism," Q&A 1.
4. Noble, *Not Your Own*, 153.

## Life Is Secure

During her high school years, she came to learn that what her parents and teachers meant was that she could be anyone or do anything she wanted as long as she got good enough grades, achieved a high SAT score, and got into an Ivy League school. So, she did everything within her power to accomplish these goals. She studied harder than any of her friends; she did more extracurricular activities than her school counselor told her was needed to get into her number one pick for college.

Come the fall after she graduated high school, she walked onto the campus of her top college and glowed with pride. She had done everything her parents, teachers, and guidance counselors had advised, and it paid off. She was here, in the best college, studying with the smartest professors, alongside peers just like her. Yet, something began to feel off. She started feeling more fatigue than usual, she didn't have energy to go to the new student socials, she missed her parents, who were on the other side of the country, and perhaps more than ever, she felt alone.

So, she did what she had been taught to do. She sought out a professional for help. She was prescribed antidepressants and was assured that before long, she would be back to her regular self. When that didn't seem to do the trick, she began looking for help in self-improvement books, thinking, "Surely, there is something wrong with me. I just need to identify the problem and get back to work." She read the popular researcher and author Brené Brown, who says, "True belonging is the spiritual practice of believing in and belonging to yourself so deeply that you can share your most authentic self with the world and find sacredness in both being a part of something and standing alone in the wilderness."[5] "That's it," Sarah thought. "I need to learn to lean into the spiritual practice of believing in and belonging to myself. I've spent all these years relying on encouragement from others who believe in me, but I've never really believed in myself."

The next morning, while scrolling on her phone, she came across an Instagram post that read, "Be your best self today. Enroll in this self-enriching seven-week program and find the version of

---

5. Brown, *Braving the Wilderness*, 9.

yourself that you can be proud of." She fills in her information and enrolls in the program. The next week, her friend invites her to a soul cycle class to help her get out of her funk, and even though she didn't feel like going, she knew that if she wanted to stop feeling so bad, she needed to get to work. After the workout, she went out for brunch with a few friends, but she came away feeling even worse about herself because all she heard her friends talk about was the importance of networking with the right companies in order to get into the best internship program that summer. The thought hadn't even occurred to her to plan for her internship. She felt so far behind.

Before long, the panic attacks started. Sarah felt her life crumbling all around her, and she lay in bed lost in her thoughts trying to figure out where she went wrong, what step didn't she take, why she didn't feel strong enough to do what everyone expected of her. The only answer she had was, "Believe in yourself, stay positive," and "Believe in yourself, you'll get through this."

Many of us have felt what Sarah felt: insecurity, inadequacy, failure. We struggle to come to Jesus and confess that we really do belong to him, because we fear that Jesus will expose the thoughts that have nagged at us for years: we are not good enough, and if anyone knew who we really were, then no one would fully love us. Yet, the good news is that Jesus' presence doesn't just reveal that lie the devil's been whispering in our ear; rather, he shows us how deeply he loves us as we are and how he is willing to do whatever it takes for us to understand that love, too. Through the cross and resurrection, he sets us free from these fears. As Alan Noble writes, "But this much I believe to be true: to the degree that our society has largely adopted the belief that we are our own and belong to ourselves, we all feel the responsibilities of Self-Belonging. This is also true: there is another to whom we belong, and living before Him frees us from the unbearable burden of self-belonging."[6] The world teaches us to belong to ourselves, but by doing so, it creates an overwhelming pressure to perform so that the world loves us. Whereas, Jesus relieves that pressure by reclaiming us as his own

---

6. Noble, *Not Your Own*, 36.

in defeating sin and death through the power of his resurrection. Thus cementing our truest identity as secure, beloved children of God.

## REST IN JESUS' RESURRECTION

As we rest in the security of Jesus Christ, we find that his path didn't end in death but rounded the corner into life everlasting. He faced the inevitable insecurity of human life, but instead of being destroyed, he emerged victorious. This victory over death is the irony of the gospel. In Jesus' weakest moment, God reveals his most extraordinary power. He displays this power most visibly when he shows us what it means to completely release our grip on self-belonging and entrust our lives to God. It's what Eugene Peterson calls the practice of death that leads to resurrection. He writes, "We practice our death by giving up our will to live on our terms. Only in that relinquishment or renunciation are we able to practice resurrection."[7] Jesus transforms death from a dead end into a bridge to new life. This transformation is the security of resurrection.

Yet, you may be wondering why we still have to die. If Jesus has paved the way so that death no longer has the final say, then why can't we just skip over it? Is it some kind of punishment?

According to the Heidelberg Catechism, because of Jesus' death and resurrection, death is no longer a punishment but a grace. The grace is that it puts an end to our misery. The catechism reads, "Our death does not pay the debt of our sins. Rather, it ends our sinning and is our entrance into eternal life."[8] As Anne Lamott often says, "We Christians like to think of death as a major change of address."[9] The power of resurrection revolutionizes death by eliminating sin.

---

7. Peterson, *Pastor*, 290.
8. Christian Reformed Church, "Heidelberg Catechism," Q&A 42.
9. Lamott, "12 Truths."

Does that mean we can no longer grieve death? Of course not. Whenever someone we love dies, even if they are a Christian, we still grieve because we love and miss them. The more you love them, the more you'll experience grief. However, we also celebrate that they are finally free from sin, the brokenness of this world, and are present with the Lord.

Freedom from sin is where true security lies. The permeating effects of sin have led to suffering, insecurity, and worry. Christ's resurrection made freedom from sin possible because he took the full punishment of sin upon his shoulders and clothed us with his righteousness. The resurrection makes death an address change and a change of clothes. In Christ, we shed our old self and put on our new self. It's why the apostle Paul tells his churches in Ephesus and Colossae to put off the old self and put on the new self. He means that because Jesus has died and risen again, you are no longer who you used to be. God has changed you. You have been made new. You are an heir to the kingdom of God. Stop behaving like someone whose life is insecure and threatened by death. Live confidently in the security of the risen Lord, knowing that because God raised him, you will be, too!

## CONCLUSION

At the bedside of his daughter's hospital bed, Frederick Buechner knew that his Christian pilgrimage had hit a point of no return. Anorexia had taken so much of his daughter's body that he didn't even recognize her anymore. Yet, as he stood there, powerless over the situation, he felt God's silent presence. He writes about it in his book *A Crazy, Holy Grace,*

> It was a horrifying, terrifying time. Which might well have given rise to the sense of, "If there is a God, what in hell is going on? How does this kind of thing get to happen?" But instead, by grace, I had this overpowering kind of comfort. God was silent. He said nothing I could hear; he did nothing I could see. But I had this tremendous

## Life Is Secure

sense that he was doing all he could do without blowing the whole show sky-high.[10]

It seems strange to say that God is doing all he can, for God has infinite power and the ability to do whatever he wants, but I think Buechner is getting at the limits that God has chosen to exist within. Not because he has to but because he loves us. He loves us so much that he allows us to take the scenic path of life. The scenic path is slower, sometimes more arduous, and certainly less boring than the interstate highway. God graciously gave us space to be human and experience the fullness of what it means to be human. Even if being human means sitting at the hospital bedside or hanging on a cross.

Of course, when life has turned for the worse, we want God to intervene, even if it means taking away our agency. God might even want that, too. Buechner concludes his reflection on the limits of God by writing,

> As I dream him, he wants so much to be able to step in and make things right, but how can God do that without destroying what life is all about? If God started stepping in and setting things right, what happens to us? We cease to be human beings. We cease to be free. We cease to be people who can do one thing or another thing with the talents we're given. We become chess pieces on a chessboard. But I sensed the passionate restraint in the silence of God, which was both silent and yet eloquent.[11]

In God's restraint, he says exactly what needs to be said for us to live exactly how he intended.

The path of following Jesus is often one of silence. It's a path that allows for all kinds of bumps in the road. It's not the most efficient route or the most comfortable. It's the path that takes us by the most beautiful fields and rivers and the most dangerous cliffs and storms. Jesus has shown us the way forward and promises never to leave us alone. As the psalmist says, "Your word is a

---

10. Buechner, *Crazy, Holy Grace*, 29.
11. Buechner, *Crazy, Holy Grace*, 29.

lamp for my feet, a light on my path."[12] May we cling to the Word that took on flesh as we face whatever our path may bring us. All the while knowing that we belong to him who walked our path already.

---

12. Ps 119:105.

# 6

# Love Is Guaranteed

*For I am convinced that neither death nor life, neither angels nor demons, neither the present nor the future, nor any powers, neither height nor depth, nor anything else in all creation, will be able to separate us from the love of God that is in Christ Jesus our Lord.*

ROMANS 8:38–39

*For neither in heaven nor among the creatures on earth is there anyone who loves us more than Jesus Christ does.*

THE BELGIC CONFESSION

TOWARDS THE END OF Isabel Allende's novel *The Long Petal of the Sea*, Victor, the protagonist, reflects on his life at eighty. He remembers his youth, filled with the blood and despair of the Spanish Civil War, the death of his young bride, and the long journey he took alongside his new sister-in-law as a refugee to Chile. To be eligible to board the ship together, their relationship must transform from in-laws to a marriage of convenience. Although a difficult choice, Victor found that life can mold meaningful existences out of convenient circumstances.

After years of struggling with his identity as a refugee in Chile, this foreign land also becomes meaningful to him. Chile becomes his home. That is, until a military coup causes him to flee Chile for Venezuela. The day would come, however, when he'd finally be able to return to Chile, where he lived the remainder of his life in the countryside. He had little control over his life's circumstances, but as he reflected upon them, he said, "Do you know what I'm most grateful for? Love. That has marked me more than anything else."[1] Like Victor, regardless of how complex or how wonderful of a life we get to live, love is what we all long to remember more than anything else.

Love is as multifaceted as a diamond. It's difficult to synthesize into a single sentence. Yet, some of our best writers have attempted. C. S. Lewis describes love as "a steady wish for the loved person's ultimate good as far as it can be obtained."[2] Anne Lamott says, "Love is what our soul is made of, and for."[3] The apostle Paul writes, "Love never fails."[4] Whatever love is, we know it is supposed to be as sturdy as an oak tree and as consistent as a lighthouse in a storm.

Perhaps the best definition of love comes from Jesus' beloved disciple, John. In his first letter, he writes deftly, "God is love."[5] God is not just loving; he is love itself. If he were to cease being love, he would stop being God. Since we are made in God's likeness, it's no wonder we all feel an innate need for sturdy and consistent love.

Yet, love can feel elusive. We can do everything within our power to procure love, but it can slip through our fingers like grains of sand. We live in a world of conditional love. We expect conditions to be met, whether in a relationship between a parent and child, husband and wife, friends, or lovers. If the relationship conditions are unmet, the relationship becomes null and void. According to numerous studies, approximately one-fourth

1. Allende, *Long Petal*, 312.
2. Lewis, *Four Loves*, 133.
3. Lamott, *Somehow*, 10.
4. 1 Cor 13:8.
5. 1 John 4:8.

of adult Americans do not speak to at least one family member.[6] The American divorce rate hovers between 40–50 percent of all marriages.[7] Friends are more challenging to come by in our fast-paced, social media–driven world, causing a loneliness epidemic. Lovers see each other as one-night opportunities instead of potential long-term relationships. Dating apps have fueled a swipe-left culture that judges people primarily on outward appearances and sexual performance. With realities like these, it's no wonder why so many people feel like love is not guaranteed.

Yet, regardless of the statistics about broken relationships or our feelings about the conditionality of love, we all have an innate need to be loved. From the moment we enter this world, we need someone to show us enough love to feed us, bathe us, and provide us a safe place to sleep. These necessities of the first couple years of life are essential to becoming someone who can offer love to others. One 2016 UK study reported that severe parental neglect in the first two years of life has lasting damage to a child's ability to thrive, as seen in a study done on children raised in Romanian orphanages and later adopted by loving families. The study reports, "When each child was 6 years old, the researchers assessed what proportion of these adopted children was functioning 'normally'. They found that 69% of the children adopted before the age of 6 months, 43% of the children adopted between the ages of 7 months and 2 years and only 22% of the children adopted between the ages of 2 years and 3½ years were functioning normally."[8] The longer these children lived in the orphanage, the more significant their dysfunction was by the age of six. However, the earlier a loving parent adopted them, the more likely they were to thrive at six years old. Love isn't optional. We all need it. The report continues and says, "Indeed longitudinal studies have reported that a child's ability to form and maintain healthy relationships throughout life may be significantly impaired by having an insecure attachment to

6. Streep, "Parent-Child Estrangement."
7. *Psychology Today*, "Divorce."
8. Winston and Chicot, "Importance of Early Bonding," 12–14.

a primary caregiver."⁹ A secure, loving attachment with a primary caregiver is essential to becoming a person who can have lasting, healthy relationships as an adult. In other words, to love, we need to be loved.

Likewise, as children of God, we need a secure foundation of love to grow into a mature, loving relationship with him, ourselves, and others. We need a love that is guaranteed. If God's love for us is conditional, we will spend our time scurrying about through life, trying to secure his love. As Augustine, a fifth-century pastor, said, "Our hearts are restless until they find rest in Thee."¹⁰ Anxiety will always leave us exhausted and insecure in our relationship with God. Yet, in God's grace, there is another way: the way of the covenant.

## THE WAY OF THE COVENANT: DAVID

We see this covenantal way in Jesus, but we first catch a glimpse of it in David. King David is Jesus' most famous ancestor in Israel. David was Israel's great underdog: the rags to riches story; the one who overcame life's most significant obstacles; from a shepherd boy to a warrior, a wanted criminal to a king, a nobody to somebody. This was David. His predecessor, King Saul, may have killed thousands, but the people of Israel sang out, "David killed ten thousands." He's the one who slew the great giant of a Philistine named Goliath. He rose to such eminence that even the nation's capital, Jerusalem, was nicknamed "The City of David."

Yet, David was far from perfect. The sin of pride tripped him up just like it did so many other kings of Israel. After defeating the Jebusites in war and claiming Jerusalem as his capital, David sought to solidify his political regime by building a temple for Yahweh. He frames the idea to the prophet, Nathan, as a noble deed. "Here I am, living in a house of cedar, while the ark of God remains in a

---

9. Winston and Chicot, "Importance of Early Bonding," 13.
10. Augustine, *Confessions*, 1.1

tent."[11] In other words, David was living in royal comfort while his God was camping on the side of the road. Where was the justice in that? Indeed, God deserved something grand. However, God never asked David to build him a temple. God had never asked any Israelite to build him a temple. God tells David through Nathan, "Wherever I have moved with all the Israelites, did I ever say to any of their rulers whom I commanded to shepherd my people Israel, 'Why have you not built me a house of cedar?'"[12] David asked to solve a problem that God didn't have.

David's tell is asking to build a temple for Yahweh. His poker face fails him. God sees right through him to the core of the issue. David wants to build a temple because that's what all the other kings of his day did when they tried to establish their authority in their kingdom. It's similar to when Israel asked for a king. Why did they want a king? Because everyone else had one! David knew that one of the primary responsibilities of any king was to take care of the gods and provide them with a place to rest. By doing so, a king fulfilled his responsibility and secured protection for his kingdom. If the gods were in a mobile tent, they could come and go as they pleased, but if they dwelt in a temple, they were permanent. Every king wanted the gods to make their kingdoms their permanent abode. David was no exception.

Yahweh's resounding no to David's request clarifies that David will not treat Yahweh like any other god. Just because the nations built stunning temples for their gods didn't mean Yahweh wanted one. He didn't need a place to rest his head. He brought the Israelites up out of Egypt to provide them with rest. David assumed that Yahweh wanted to be treated like the gods of other nations, but this assumption exposed his lack of understanding of who Yahweh was.

Yet, instead of taking the kingdom away from David, as he did with Saul, Yahweh graciously reminds David of his divine identity. Yahweh is the God who transforms weakness into strength. He made an unknown shepherd boy into a Goliath-slaying warrior.

11. 2 Sam 7:2.
12. 2 Sam 7:7.

He established David's throne when, just days before, he was living with the Philistines, hiding from King Saul. God specializes in unlikely situations.

Therefore, God proves himself again to David by showering him with extravagant promises. God promises to establish David's kingdom forever. David's reign will never end; it will live on throughout his generations. One of his descendants will even be able to build God a temple. And when that descendent disobeys God, he will be punished, "But my love will never be taken away from him."[13] God's response to David's bullheaded request to build him a temple guarantees love.

This moment in Israel's history can quickly be glossed over, but it is one of the most significant interactions between God and his people in the Old Testament. God gave his people every opportunity to follow his laws, enjoy the rest he offered, and live faithfully before him. Time and again, they failed, from the time of the judges, when everyone did what was right in their own eyes, to the days of Samuel, when Israel asked for a king. God's people could not get their act together, and neither could David. Yet, instead of rejecting them, God changed the dynamic by offering an unconditional covenant of love. God says, "I've given you more than you can imagine. I know that won't produce obedience. So, I want you to know that even when you disobey, I still love you. I wholeheartedly commit to you and will never abandon you." God's sturdy and consistent love becomes the foundation of his relationship with his people.

## THE WAY OF THE COVENANT: JESUS

God's guarantee of love is no abstraction and became concrete in the incarnation of Jesus Christ. This babe, born to a peasant in Bethlehem, highlighted God's counterintuitive way of loving in the world. Instead of descending on Israel as their righteous king, ready to slay the enemy of Rome, God took the form of a helpless

---

13. 2 Sam 7:15.

baby who lived under Rome's thumb. However, this baby grew up and lived unlike anyone who had ever lived before. He did not allow resentments to fester, selfish ambition to run wild, or lustful desires to overwhelm him. Instead, he followed all of God's laws. He loved the weakest and most vulnerable around him as if they were the wealthiest and most powerful. He never disobeyed his Father in heaven. Such obedience surely deserves to be rewarded with a crown. Yet, instead of a coronation, he was crowned at a crucifixion. The weight of that crown contained humanity's complete hatred of God. God unveiled his glory as the thorns pierced deeper into Jesus' skull. God's pinnacle of power was the world's idea of utter failure. Beaten, bloody, and bludgeoned are not exactly words that describe power, might, or strength. Yet, this is precisely the way God revealed who he is. His power shone forth because the crucifixion gave way to the resurrection.

Jesus' resurrection is God's guarantee of love for the whole world. His resurrection proved that though the penalty of sin is death, life beyond the grave is possible. From a human perspective, death is the worst thing that can happen because it means the end of hope, love, and life itself. As I heard my wife, Annie, say in a prayer regarding the death of a young person, "The worst thing has happened." Yet, because of Jesus' resurrection, death is no longer the end but the beginning of eternal life. He changed death from a coffin to a doorway and beckoned us, "Come." Love will always be on offer to us because Jesus has made "a way out of no way." His love cannot be defeated. "Nothing can separate us from the love of God in Jesus Christ."[14]

Jesus is our rescuer because God rescued him. When we are on death's doorstep, we naturally cry out to God for help, and his response is the living Christ. The church father, Augustine, described the impulse to be rescued by God in a prayer,

> Say to my soul, "I myself am your rescue." Say it in such a way that I hear it. Here before you are the ears with which my heart hears, Master. Open them and say to my soul, "I myself am your rescue." I will run after the sound

14. Rom 8:9.

of your voice and lay hold of you. Do not hide your face from me. Let me die, to keep me from dying, and let me see your face.[15]

The paradoxical rescue that God offers in Jesus Christ is rescue that comes through death.

So, yes, it's true; nothing can separate us from the love of God in Jesus Christ. When we can learn to rest in this beautiful mystery, we won't be able to stop ourselves from seeking after Jesus. As the Catholic theologian Hans Urs von Balthasar wrote,

> There is in love an eagerness which wants to get to know the beloved, to explore him, observe him from all sides. And there is one reason why the Word of God becomes flesh—to allow himself to be gazed upon and touched in this way, out of love for the Father.[16]

God is love, and he revealed his love in the face of Jesus Christ.

The love that God guarantees in Jesus' resurrection is the kind of love that changes lives. It's a love that responds to every sin with "Be healed. Go and sin no more." Change through love occurs all the time in recovery groups around the world. If you attend any twelve-step group for Alcoholics Anonymous, you'll see a group of people who have learned to imitate God's love for the sinner. When a member of the group shares about a recent relapse, there is no response of shaming or blaming. Instead, there is a gracious and loving response. Members say, "I'm so impressed that you showed up today and are still choosing recovery. Your story of relapse and recovery is helping my recovery today." This kind of unconditional love and acceptance inspires the recently relapsed alcoholic to put away the liquor and keep coming back to the meetings.

Only love will ultimately motivate us to live changed lives. Jesus says there is no greater love than the one who lays down his life for his friends. Admittedly, the church is not always where people experience unconditional love. In many churches, people feel like they have to put a better version of themselves forward so that the

---

15. Augustine, *Confessions*, 1.7.5.
16. Balthasar, *Heart of the World*.

church will accept them. They don't feel comfortable or invited to confess the messiness of their lives or their most egregious sins. Countless people describe the church as a place where they can't be themselves. That's a shame because Jesus only ever welcomes us as we are. When we encounter him, we can't help but be changed because, as the blind man says, "I was blind, but now I see."[17]

## CONCLUSION

The resurrected love of Jesus Christ is the only love strong enough to be guaranteed under the pangs of death. Christian Wiman reflects on the death of Gerard Manley Hopkins in his book *My Bright Abyss: Meditation of a Modern Believer*. Gerard Manley Hopkins was a poet and priest who died of typhoid at forty-five. His last words were, "I am so happy. I am so happy. I loved my life."[18] Wiman writes, "To die well, even for the atheist, is to believe that there is some way of dying into life rather than simply away from it, some form of survival that love makes possible. I don't mean by survival merely persisting in the memory of others. I mean something deeper and more durable."[19] Wiman discovered that more durable kind of love as he sat by his grandmother's deathbed. He writes that "her every tear was wiped away, that God looked her out of pain, that in the blink of an eye the world opened its tenderest interiors, and let her in."[20] Fear did not mark Wiman's grandmother's death. Instead, God's great love filled her soul.

There is no better example of the love that Wiman describes as "dying into life" than Jesus Christ. Jesus died, was set free from all pain, tears, and suffering, and was exalted to the glory of a king. As Herman Bavinck writes, "Death, as it were, ensnared Christ with its pangs, but those pangs were the labor pains of the resurrection, which would be undone by God in the moment of resurrection.

17. John 9:25.
18. Wiman, *Bright Abyss*, loc. 40.
19. Wiman, *Bright Abyss*, loc. 40.
20. Wiman, *Bright Abyss*, loc. 42.

And thus, in God's good pleasure, Christ became the firstborn from the dead. His resurrection was a birth from death and hence a victory over death and over him who had the power of death, the devil."[21] The pain we carry throughout life like a backpack full of bricks is not a permanent fixture. Jesus' resurrection exemplifies a love that guarantees freedom from the burdens of sin, suffering, and death.

---

21. Bavinck, *Sin and Salvation*, 438.

# PART 3: CHRIST WILL COME AGAIN

# 7

# The Spirit Is with Us

*Do you not know that your bodies are temples of the Holy Spirit, who is in you, whom you have received from God?*

1 CORINTHIANS 6:19-20

*Listening to the Spirit is not an archaeological dig for some original deposit but rather an attunement to a God with us, still speaking, still surprising, still revealing.*

JAMES K. A. SMITH, *HOW TO INHABIT TIME*

THE THREAT OF ABANDONMENT triggers some of our most basic survival instincts. When these instincts are triggered, we often become willing to do whatever it takes to keep our most valued relationships in place. Pixar provides a vivid telling of this fear in *Toy Story 3*. Woody and Buzz's loving kid, Andy, has grown up and is moving to college. He has been their trusted protector and friend for as long as they can remember. He has shown them that no matter how many new toys he gets, he will always have a special place in his heart for them.

Woody is unrelentingly committed to Andy. He stands ready to do whatever Andy needs from him, even if that means sitting in the attic indefinitely while Andy is away at college. Buzz, on the other hand, is open to different possibilities. He accepts that their playing days with Andy have come to a natural conclusion. He's ready for the next chapter, the next kid.

Woody crosses his arms. He's not going to abandon Andy. Andy is not going to abandon him. Throughout the movie, he goes to extreme lengths to be the toy he thinks Andy needs. At one point, things get so out of hand that Woody willingly abandons his closest friends and gets caught in an incinerator that looks like the depths of hell.[1]

Abandonment is a terrifying reality. We all need secure and reliable relationships with those who love us. It's an innate human need to be comforted by friends and family who will not leave us. And yet, some of us know from experience that those closest to us are not always there when we need them to be. Sometimes, our kids move to college, our parents die, and our friends don't stay in touch. We are not guaranteed tomorrow, and neither are our loved ones. We tend to live like Woody, doing whatever it takes or being whoever we need to be to ensure those closest to us don't abandon us.

Jesus' disciples felt this fear acutely in their relationship with Jesus. In a conversation about Jesus' relationship with the Father, the disciples realize that Jesus plans to leave them to return to his Father sooner than expected. Can you imagine being Jesus' disciples and hearing these words? His disciples gave up everything to follow Jesus. They left their careers, their families, and their communities. They watched Jesus rebuke the day's religious leaders and perform massive miracles: raising the dead, giving sight to the blind, making the lame walk, and even watching him cross cultural barriers by talking to and caring for Samaritans. Jesus was their fearless leader, hero, and rock; how could he think of leaving them? I mean, he was only in his early thirties. Was it time to throw in the towel and quit the best ministry ever coming to the

1. Unkrich, *Toy Story 3*.

Mediterranean world? They knew they couldn't do this work on their own. They couldn't imagine it without Jesus.

When push comes to shove, Peter refuses to let Jesus go. As the mob of soldiers and religious leaders led by Judas approach Jesus, he doesn't hesitate. He pulls out his shortsword from his belt and reacts violently. The blood soaks the dusty ground before he can give it a second thought. His violence was new to him, but he couldn't let them take Jesus. He knew it was worth it, even if it took cutting off an ear. Yet, to Peter's surprise, Jesus took a few steps towards the injured man and picked up his freshly severed ear. Without so much as a needle and thread, he molded the ear back onto his skull with the skill of a master sculptor. Jesus didn't need Peter's protection. He had another plan.

Jesus meets Peter's fear of abandonment with a comforting vision of God making his home in Peter's body. Instead of abandoning anyone, Jesus promises that God is drawing closer than ever before. In John 14:18, Jesus says, "I will not leave you as orphans." An orphan is categorically abandoned. Jesus promises his disciples that abandonment is not in their future. Their future is secure in his presence.

## JESUS IS MADE PRESENT BY THE HOLY SPIRIT

Jesus' presence, however, will not be in flesh and blood; instead, he will be mediated to them by the Holy Spirit. "I will ask the Father, and he will give you another advocate to help you and be with you forever—the Spirit of truth."[2] This advocate is not less than Jesus but is equal to and fully united with Jesus and the Father. As the apostle Paul writes in Gal 4:6, "Because you are his sons, God sent the Spirit of his Son into our hearts, the Spirit who calls out, 'Abba, Father.'" The triune God works in tandem as he makes his presence known in our lives.

The Holy Spirit is closer to us than our breath, but there is confusion about his role in our lives for many of us. In my tradition,

2. John 14:16.

we tend to hear more about God the Father and the Son. Many of us tend to put God the Holy Spirit on the back burner. There is a hesitancy in becoming too familiar with the Spirit because of the Spirit's associations with the charismatic movement. The charismatic movement began in the early 1900s in Los Angeles. It emphasized the use of spiritual gifts and baptism with the Holy Spirit. It is most famous for its practice of speaking in tongues. It eventually became a global movement and can be found in almost every major branch of Christianity. Although the charismatic movement has its strengths, like integrating faith and emotions, it has left a lot of Christians wondering, "If I don't speak in tongues, if I don't have faith that heals, if I don't see the Spirit at work, then am I a *real* Christian?" These questions are the open door that insecurity needs to derail one's faith.

I spoke with a gas station attendant about the Christian faith during my first year of college. It turns out that he was a Christian and actively involved in his church community. To my surprise, shortly into our conversation, he asked me, "Do you speak in tongues?" I was confused as to why he wanted to know about this, but after saying no, he quickly told me, "If you don't speak in tongues, you are not a Christian." I left the conversation discouraged and frustrated. I knew that the Holy Spirit's role in my life was more significant than the singular spiritual gift of tongues, but I didn't know what that looked like at the time.

## THE HOLY SPIRIT'S STORY

The Holy Spirit first appears in the Bible in the Genesis creation account. He's depicted as hovering over the waters like a helicopter, his calm breath rippling over the chaos of the sea. This juxtaposition emphasizes God's power over creation. In the ancient world, people associated water with chaos. Nobody could tame it. Yet, the waters didn't stand a chance when God's Spirit showed up. The Spirit is the master over chaos.

God's Spirit brings order out of chaos because he is God's breath. The Hebrew word for Spirit is *rûaḥ*, which means "spirit," "breath," or "wind." So, just as God created the world by his very breath, he breathed life into Adam. Genesis 2:7 reads, "Then the LORD God formed a man from the dust of the ground and breathed into his nostrils the breath of life, and the man became a living being." Although this sounds like the original version of CPR, there is something theologically happening here. The breath of life is God's life imparted to humanity. Unlike the many creation myths of the ancient Near East, Genesis depicts a God who creates humanity to image him, not to be his slaves. Humanity is born out of who God is. Each breath ought to remind us that without the Spirit's breath in our lungs, we have no life.

Therefore, Jesus' promise to the disciples that they would be filled with the Spirit was good news. The very source of life would be theirs. Ever since Adam and Eve left the garden of Eden, God has been on a mission to walk with his people again in the cool of the day. In the days of Israel, God dwelled with his people using the tabernacle and the temple. By moving into disciples' bodies, the Holy Spirit transforms ordinary bodies into temples of the most high God. The apostle Paul writes about these temples in 1 Cor 6:19-20: "Do you not know that your bodies are temples of the Holy Spirit, who is in you, whom you have received from God? You are not your own; you were bought at a price. Therefore, honor God with your bodies." The Spirit's presence in the human body makes it all the more imperative to honor God with one's body. In Paul's day, he was writing about honoring God with your body through your sex life, but we could apply his words to many areas of our lives: relationships, health, work, etc. Our bodies are not only precious because we are God's image-bearers but because we are his home. So, God is involved with our bodies wherever we go and whatever we do with them.

Ultimately, we see Jesus' words come true in Acts 2, as the Spirit descends on the disciples and many others, but what is more interesting is what Jesus says the Spirit will do. "On that day, [the day the Spirit comes] you will realize that I am in my Father, and you are in me, and I am in you."[3] In other words, when Jesus has

---

3. John 14:20.

risen from the dead and the Holy Spirit has descended, the disciples will understand the true nature of their relationship with Jesus. They aren't just followers of God but also members of God's family. They are intrinsically linked to Jesus by the Holy Spirit in the same way that Jesus is one with the Father.

Jesus and the Father are two distinct persons united in an eternal loving relationship. Jesus shares this bond with his disciples, who need the Spirit to experience the great intimacy he wants to have with them. Death can't defeat this intimacy, and no amount of time or distance can cause it to fizzle out. It is of the exact nature as Jesus' relationship with the Father.

Jesus describes this intimacy in shocking terms. While teaching in a synagogue in Capernaum, he emphatically states, "Very truly I tell you, unless you eat the flesh of the Son of Man and drink his blood, you have no life in you."[4] Just as we need food and drink to survive each day, we need Jesus' body and blood to endure eternally. We need Jesus in us to live beyond the grave.

Jesus' words hearken back to God breathing life into Adam. Adam didn't just need working organs, a skeleton, and skin; instead, he needed God to show up and be the life he needed. God's Spirit is Adam's life source, and he is how we partake in the body and blood of Christ.

The connection between Jesus' teaching and the sacrament of the Lord's Supper has been a point of controversy throughout church history. During the Protestant Reformation, there were many debates about how exactly Jesus' body and blood could be in the bread and wine of the Supper. Roman Catholics argue that the Holy Spirit transforms the bread and wine into the body and blood of Christ. Lutherans contend that the Holy Spirit does not transform the elements but rather that Jesus surrounds them and feeds us himself. Reformed Christians argue that Christ remains at the Father's right hand but still nourishes us by the power of the Holy Spirit. Still others think of Jesus' words as metaphorical and defend a memorial view of the Supper, i.e., we remember Jesus' body and blood as we partake in the bread and wine. Whatever

4. John 6:53.

view one agrees with, what is most important is that Jesus is more intimately connected to us than we can imagine because of the Holy Spirit. He has become part of us.

The Spirit-forged bond we have with Jesus Christ also means that what is said of Jesus is said of us. Jesus is distinct from the Father, yet he is one with the Father. Likewise, Christians are not Jesus, but we are one with Jesus. As the Heidelberg Catechism explains, the Spirit "makes me share in Christ and all of his benefits."[5] Jesus pours himself out so that all that is his becomes ours. Paul puts it succinctly in Rom 8,

> And if the Spirit of him who raised Jesus from the dead is living in you, he who raised Christ from the dead will also give life to your mortal bodies because of his Spirit who lives in you. . . . The Spirit himself testifies with our spirit that we are God's children. Now if we are children, then we are heirs—heirs of God and co-heirs with Christ, if indeed we share in his sufferings in order that we may also share in his glory.[6]

Through the Spirit's work, we share Jesus' inheritance as a child of God. By leaving the disciples, Jesus makes room for them to join him in his kingdom one day.

As the Holy Spirit performs his primary role of mediating Christ to us, we experience true comfort in his presence. The Holy Spirit is not a tool; he is a person. Just as Jesus and the Father are persons, so is the Holy Spirit. His role in our lives provides absolute comfort and encouragement to us. In Acts 9:31, Luke concludes the story of Saul's conversion and persecution in the church by saying, "Then the church throughout Judea, Galilee, and Samaria enjoyed a time of peace and was strengthened. Living in the fear of the Lord and encouraged by the Holy Spirit, it increased in numbers." The Holy Spirit sustained the early church even amid growing tension and persecution. The presence of God is precisely what we need in times of distress.

---

5. Christian Reformed Church, "Heidelberg Catechism," Q&A 53.
6. Rom 8:11, 16–17.

## CONCLUSION

I underestimated the power of presence until the day after my mother-in-law passed away. We were at my father-in-law's house in Wisconsin. No one knew what we should do, but there was one person who brought an immense amount of comfort amid such heartache. It was our uncle, Jeff. Uncle Jeff drove up to the hospital to be with my father-in-law after my mother-in-law died. He then caravaned home with him, staying with us all day. He didn't say anything spectacular; he didn't do anything in particular, but he was present. He didn't let the awkwardness or the discomfort scare him away. Amid our pain, he remained present. His abiding presence was a work of the Holy Spirit in him. He became Jesus' hands and feet for us amid grief.

The Spirit is present in us. As we live each day, God lives within us. As we go about our tasks, God goes with us. As we love others, God is working through us. The Spirit frees us from the need or urge to become good enough for God. The Spirit frees us from the need to be good enough for other people. The Spirit frees us from the need to be good enough for ourselves. Instead, the Spirit bears his fruit in us as a thanksgiving offering to God. He bears the fruit of love, joy, peace, patience, kindness, goodness, faithfulness, gentleness, and self-control.[7] He assures us that we belong in body and in spirit to Jesus Christ, that we are beloved daughters and sons of God. Jesus may have returned to heaven, but his presence continues to permeate our lives by the power of the Holy Spirit.

---

7. Gal 5:22–23.

# 8

# Our Flesh Is in God's Presence

*Therefore, since we have a great high priest who has ascended into heaven, Jesus the Son of God, let us hold firmly to the faith we profess. For we do not have a high priest who is unable to empathize with our weaknesses, but we have one who has been tempted in every way, just as we are—yet he did not sin. Let us then approach God's throne of grace with confidence, so that we may receive mercy and find grace to help us in our time of need.*

HEBREWS 4:14–16

*The ascension of Christ in this sense is his exaltation to glory and power but through the cross, certainly an exaltation from humiliation to royal majesty, but through crucifixion and sacrifice, for the power and glory of the royal priest is bound up with his self-sacrifice in death and resurrection.*

T. F. TORRANCE, *ATONEMENT*

MY PHONE RANG SHORTLY after seven o'clock in the morning. The sun had barely peeked through the darkness when I heard Dennis's mother on the other end of the line. Two policemen had shown up at their door with an outstanding warrant for Dennis's arrest. They took Dennis into custody, and he waited to be arraigned at the nearby courthouse. She was at home with his two young sons.

As I opened the large wooden door into the courtroom, I looked around at a world of anxiety: mothers, fathers, brothers, sisters, and friends waiting for their loved ones to be called before the judge. A police officer stood against the right wall and reminded people to turn off their phones. There was a hush in the room as the judge took his seat, and the proceedings began. One young man after another was brought before the judge. The judge had a gentle tone to his voice. He seemed experienced, and it seemed as though he wanted the best for these young men. He read them their rights and reminded them that if they could not afford an attorney, the state would appoint one for them and set their bail. Before long, I saw Dennis walk out of the back door with a sullen look. Everything inside of me wanted to stand up and plead his case, but there was nothing I could do. The judge read Dennis the riot act within two minutes, and a police officer led him out of the courtroom.

After making bail, Dennis was back home with his mother and sons. Before long, we were back to our usual routine of meeting up for lunch, and he continued to help me out around the church. Several weeks later, he was standing before the same judge. I was sitting in the same seat, but an attorney pleaded Dennis's case this time. Dennis was short on cash, so a state-appointed attorney had to do it. The attorney convinced the judge to let Dennis off with some required anger management classes in less than a minute. With little court experience, I was shocked by how quickly the process moved. It made me wonder how much more the attorney could have done if she had more time and skin in the game. How much more would she have fought if she was in the place of the perpetrator?

When Jesus ascended back to his Father's right hand in heaven, he committed himself to be our eternal advocate in God's presence. As our advocate, Jesus not only took the punishment for our sins but also defends our case before the Father, declaring humanity is worthy of his love because we are united to Jesus. "Who then is the one who condemns? No one. Christ Jesus who died—more than that, who was raised to life—is at the right hand of God and is also interceding for us."[1] It's as if after a week of showing up late to the office, missing deadlines, and not meeting your sales quota, your boss went before the CEO and told her why you're his best employee and why you should be given a promotion. Jesus is eternally advocating on sinners' behalf before the Father, giving him every reason why we are welcomed in his presence, even though apart from Christ, we are unworthy.

## AN EMBODIED ASCENSION

Forty days after his resurrection, when Jesus returned to heaven, he did not look the way he did when he left to be born in a manger. He reentered heaven with skin on. Not just any skin, but our skin. As the resurrected Christ, he has accepted this flesh for the rest of eternity. He has willingly confined himself to the dimensions of a human body for our sake. So, unlike Dennis's lawyer, our advocate in heaven is investing the rest of eternity into our case and has all his skin in the game. "The Ascension was from one standpoint the restoration of the glory that the Son had before the Incarnation, from another the glorifying of human nature in a way that had never happened before, and from a third the start of a reign that had not previously been exercised in this form."[2] Jesus' bodily form in heaven is a guarantee that our bodies will be accepted as well. As he says to his disciples, "My Father's house has many rooms; if that were not so, would I have told you that I am going there to prepare a place for you? And if I go and prepare a place for you, I will come back and take you to be with me that you also may be where I am."[3] The good news of Jesus' ascension is that our flesh

---

1. Rom 8:34.
2. Packer, *Concise Theology*, 127.
3. John 14:2–3.

has been accepted in God's presence because *Jesus* is accepted in God's presence.

One of the benefits of being united to Jesus Christ is that even though we are not physically present in heaven with him yet, we already are spiritually. The connection between us and Jesus is never severed. Paul explains, "God raised us up with Christ and seated us with him in the heavenly realms in Christ Jesus."[4] Some theologians have described this connection as a mystical union.[5] This relationship that transcends space may be difficult for us to understand, but we are in good company, even the disciples had their hesitations about Jesus. "Then the eleven disciples went to Galilee, to the mountain where Jesus had told them to go. When they saw him, they worshiped him; but some doubted."[6] The disciples held their worship and doubts in tension. Wesley Hill comments, "If even the ones who saw the risen Jesus on a mountainside in Galilee could struggle to believe, then we too can breathe a bit easier, knowing that when we doubt, we're in good company and no worse off than the first generation of Christian believers."[7] Doubts are a normal part of the Christian journey and even as we doubt, Jesus continues to work on our behalf.

## OUR ASCENDED PRIEST

As our advocate, Jesus fulfills the priestly role found throughout the Scriptures. God called Israel's priests to be the middlemen between him and his people. If God showed up in all of his glory, his people would not survive the sight of him.[8] The priest, however, was given extraordinary access to God and served as a representative of the people. God invited the priest to enter his presence and make sacrifices on behalf of his sins as well as the sins of the

---

4. Eph 2:6.
5. See Nevin, *Mystical Presence*.
6. Matt 28:16–17.
7. Hill, *Easter*, 88.
8. Exod 19:20–22.

people. Yet, even the priests experienced God's wrath if they drew near to God without his authorization.[9] Therefore, the priests went to great lengths to confirm that God would welcome them into his presence, including making animal sacrifices, wearing particular clothing, and washing themselves.[10] The priestly role always required acute attention to both God and the people.

Israel's priests, however, were far from perfect. They felt threatened by the leadership's power and began to revolt.[11] They felt like Moses was lording his power over them and treating them like his slaves. Later on, the prophet Hosea even accuses them of murdering helpless people.[12] Eventually, this unfaithfulness of the priests and the people led to God's glory departing the temple.[13] Much like when Adam and Eve first sinned or like the people of Noah's day had turned away from God towards violence, Israel yet again turned away from God, and God responded unequivocally. The whole Old Testament story seems to teach that unless God takes up the role of priest, there is no hope for atonement between him and his people. They will continue in this cycle unless God intervenes.

God fulfills the priestly role through Jesus Christ. Jesus is the new and better priest. He obeys in every way we do not,[14] he does not fall prey to temptation,[15] and he teaches the people to do the same.[16] Since Jesus does not need to sacrifice for his own sins, he is the perfect sacrifice for the world's sins. Although it was the soldiers nailing his wrists to the cross, he was only there because, as the priest, he was offering a sacrifice on behalf of the people. Like the lamb took the punishment for sins in the Old Testament, Jesus took the final judgment for sin as his wounds poured out blood,

9. Lev 10:1–3.
10. Lev 16.
11. Num 16.
12. Hos 6:9.
13. Ezek 10.
14. Matt 3:15.
15. Matt 4.
16. Matt 5–7.

and he breathed his last. He was both the priest and the sacrifice. Jesus did what no priest had ever done before.

In Jesus' work on the cross, he received the punishment for sin, but it didn't solve the age-old impossibility of humans standing in God's presence. When Jesus died, people didn't stop sinning. They kept on living as they always had. They were just as unworthy to stand before God as they were before Jesus was born. Three days after his death, he reappeared in the same body, but God had made it new. He still bore the scars on his wrists and side from the crucifixion, but he had gone through the ultimate baptism in his death, and he came out completely new. This new, resurrected body is the key to bridging the final divide between God and humanity. Jesus' resurrected flesh could withstand the awesome glory of God in heaven. Therefore, John wrote, "My dear children, I write this to you so that you will not sin. But if anybody does sin, we have an advocate with the Father—Jesus Christ, the Righteous One."[17] Our advocate is the sinless Son of God.

During Jesus' earthly ministry, he foreshadows the glory of his resurrected and ascended body. He leads a few of his disciples on a hike up a high mountain, where he is transfigured before them. "His face shone like the sun, and his clothes became as white as the light."[18] The disciples must have thought something was wrong with their vision because they didn't know what they were seeing. Peter frantically responds by offering to build a tent, but just then, like when John baptized Jesus, a voice from heaven says, "This is my Son, whom I love; with him I am well pleased. Listen to him!"[19] The transfiguration is a taste of the the incarnate son of God unconditionally loved and welcomed in God's presence.

---

17. 1 John 2:1.
18. Matt 17:2.
19. Matt 17:5.

## OUR ASCENDED KING

When Jesus ascended to the Father, he was not only welcomed by God, but given a seat at his right hand. The same place where he dwelt before he became human was the place his Father welcomed him back into. The right hand of God is a symbol of Jesus' full authority as divine king. Paul even uses Jesus' seat in heaven as the Christian's true north in life, saying,

> Since, then, you have been raised with Christ, set your hearts on things above, where Christ is, seated at the right hand of God. Set your minds on things above, not on earthly things. For you died, and your life is now hidden with Christ in God. When Christ, who is your life, appears, then you also will appear with him in glory.[20]

The eternal Son of God in human flesh is sitting on his throne in perfect reconciliation between divinity and humanity. He accomplished his primary task of bringing humanity back into God's presence. Therefore, set your hearts on him because God's presence is the place where all of our deepest needs are provided for.

## CONCLUSION

In Wendell Berry's novel *Hannah Coulter*, the main character, Hannah, feels pain like a dagger in her chest as her three children grow up and move away from their family farm. She is happy for them to go to college, get an education, get married, and have their own children, but she dreams about one of them taking over the farm. She longs for them to see the fields and pastures they grew up playing on as their own land.

After her daughter's divorce, her grandson began coming to the farm every weekend and spending his summer vacations there. She begins to feel hope kindle again in her heart. The joy in her grandson's eyes becomes her joy as he follows her husband around

---

20. Col 3:1–4.

the farm, baling hay, caring for the animals, and doing odd jobs around the house. Surely, he was her legacy.

Yet, as he got older, he began to be pulled away from the farm by the attractions of the city, friends, and a part-time job. Hannah didn't know exactly when it happened, but eventually, the phone stopped ringing, and his car didn't come down the driveway. Her hope for the future began fading like a photo exposed to too much sun. Hannah didn't know what she was waiting for as the years passed. She says,

> Here in Port William, it seems, we are waiting. For what? For the last of the old rememberers and the old memories to disappear forever? For the coming of knowledge that will make us a community again? For the catastrophe that will force us to become a community again? For the catastrophe that will end everything? For the Second Coming?[21]

What she didn't know was that she was still waiting for her grandson, until one night, he showed up, "He looked like death warmed over, and his face was wet with tears. He looked like a man who had been lost at sea and had made it to shore at last, but had barely made it."[22] After inviting him in and telling him to call his mother to tell her where he was and that he loved her, Hannah asked, "Well, what brings you back?" He said, "I want to be here. I want to live here and farm. It's the only thing I really want to do. I found that out."[23]

After trying everything the world had to offer to heal the wounds of his childhood and his parent's divorce, he came to the end of himself and realized his grandmother's farm always had what he needed to find restoration. As he got back into the rhythm of the farm, Hannah noticed that he slowly got his confidence back in his eyes, but it wasn't until one night when he returned from a long day on the farm and told her a long story and together they had a good laugh that she knew he'd be all right.

21. Berry, *Hannah Coulter*, 181.
22. Berry, *Hannah Coulter*, 182.
23. Berry, *Hannah Coulter*, 183.

## Our Flesh Is in God's Presence

When we are anxiety-ridden or depressed, we don't have the bandwidth for laughter, yet when we get rest, when we know deep in our bones, that we are secure, we can begin to let go of our worries and enjoy life again. As we show up in heaven and see Jesus sitting in our flesh at the Father's right hand in all his glory, we will experience rest unlike anything we've felt before. We will feel at ease in God's presence, knowing that there in God's throne room was the healing we had been longing for our whole lives. How will we be able to do anything but laugh with joy, just as Hannah did with her grandson?

# 9

# Judgment Is a Comfort

*Therefore judge nothing before the appointed time; wait until the Lord comes. He will bring to light what is hidden in darkness and will expose the motives of the heart. At that time each will receive their praise from God.*

1 CORINTHIANS 4:5

Q. *How does Christ's return "to judge the living and the dead" comfort you?*
A. *In all distress and persecution, with an uplifted head, I confidently await the very judge who has already offered himself to the judgment of God in my place and removed the whole curse from me. Christ will cast all his enemies and mine into everlasting condemnation, but will take me and all his chosen ones to himself into the joy and glory of heaven.*

HEIDELBERG CATECHISM Q&A 52

WHEN LIZZIE WAS 101 years old, she suffered excruciating pain in her legs. All she could do was lie in bed or sit in her recliner. She couldn't enjoy the cool autumn breeze on her face or walk in her old neighborhood, relishing the changing colors. All she could do

## Judgment Is a Comfort

was sit and think. So, she had a lot on her mind when I pulled up a small wooden desk chair next to her recliner. Once a cheerful aging woman, she now felt depressed and scared about her future. Tears filled her eyes as she confessed to me, "All this pain must be God's judgment on me because I've not always been a good person. There are so many people that I've hurt, and I've never made amends with them." I attempted to comfort her by reminding her that by her age, physical pain is normal, but it was no use. Lizzie was overwhelmed with feelings of guilt, shame, and fear.

Lizzie is not alone in thinking God's judgment is brought about through physical pain. For many years, I also considered physical pain a sign of God at work in me. God was directing me to confess sin, be generous with my time or money, or helping me to make a decision. This may sound odd to some, but in the fundamentalist Christian culture I grew up in, this was normal. I assumed I was like Job, suffering some kind of divine test of faith. Yet, as I became an adult, I learned that much of my pain was a symptom of anxiety. After going to therapy, starting some anti-anxiety medications, and making some behavioral changes, the pain went away. It was such a relief. Yet, without the pain, I had to learn how to relate to God in new ways.

One of the ways that has helped me to relate to God anew is remembering and reflecting on my secure future in him. In our therapeutic culture, we spend much time thinking about our past. We attend talk therapy and reflect on how we were traumatized as children. We wonder not only about ourselves but also about how our parents might have been traumatized and then their parents, too. The therapist tells us that the past is the key to unlocking the present. But is that the whole truth? Of course, as a recipient of therapy, I've benefited considerably from reflecting deeply with a professional therapist about my story and how the wounds of my childhood affect the way I behave and think today, but what about the future? As a Christian, I believe that one day God will judge the living and the dead. How might that future open up more room for healing and hope in my life today?

As a pastor in the Dutch Reformed tradition, I often look to the Heidelberg Catechism for clarity and insights on theological issues. If you ask anyone who has spent time in the catechism, you'll usually hear how much the first question and answer means to them. Instead of focusing on the purpose of life or some theological doctrine like many other catechisms and confessions, the Heidelberg Catechism begins with a focus on comfort by asking, "What is your only comfort in life and in death?" The short answer is simply, "That I am not my own, but belong—body and soul in life and in death—to my faithful savior, Jesus Christ."[1] The first answer in this catechism captures the hearts of many of its readers. We long to be comforted by our savior, Jesus Christ.

Many readers of the Heidelberg Catechism don't realize that the theme of comfort runs through the catechism. Surprisingly, it even says the future that we are either terrified of or don't understand is a comfort to believers today. Question and answer 52 reads, "How does Christ's return 'to judge the living and the dead' comfort you? In all distress and persecution, with an uplifted head, I confidently await the very judge who has already offered himself to the judgment of God in my place and removed the whole curse from me. Christ will cast all his enemies and mine into everlasting condemnation, but will take me and all his chosen ones to himself into the joy and glory of heaven."[2] The return of Christ and his judgment comforts us because it secures our future and promises that justice will have the final say.

## A SECURE FUTURE

Our future is secure because Jesus already took the judgment upon himself. God's judgment has already been accomplished because the penalty for sin has been paid and new life has been given. We need not rely on what we did or didn't accomplish in our lifetime to prove ourselves worthy to God. As Fleming Rutledge writes, "We

---

1. Christian Reformed Church, "Heidelberg Catechism," Q&A 1.
2. Christian Reformed Church, "Heidelberg Catechism," Q&A 52.

## Judgment Is a Comfort

cannot rely on any known good deeds; the complete astonishment of the redeemed and the shattered confidence of the condemned are clear evidence of this."[3] Yet, we can rely on the deeds of the judge. His sacrifice and righteousness is what brings us through judgment and into life.

In Jesus' last words of teaching to his disciples before his friend, Judas, betrays him, he teaches them that their actions will never live up to God's standards. He does this by talking about the sheep and the goats. "When the Son of Man comes in his glory, and all the angels with him, he will sit on his glorious throne. All the nations will be gathered before him, and he will separate the people one from another as a shepherd separates the sheep from the goats. He will put the sheep on his right and the goats on his left."[4] Jesus paints a breathtaking picture of the final day of justice, when all people will stand before him and be exposed for all to see. As the Episcopal priest Fleming Rutledge describes,

> He will sit on his throne of glory, and at his feet, spread out before him, will be all of human history in unimaginable completeness. Julius Caesar and Napoleon will be there; Genghis Khan and Joan of Arc will be there; Martin Luther and Catherine the Great and Voltaire and Stalin will be there. . . . The impression burned into our hearts today is this: on the climatic and final day, we will be there.[5]

That is both a glorious and a terrifying picture. Along with all the world's people, we will stand before God's majestic throne in awe of his power and greatness. But we will also see more clearly than ever how far we fall short of his glory. As Jesus says, "The King will reply, 'Truly I tell you, whatever you did for one of the least of these brothers and sisters of mine, you did for me.'"[6] Jesus connects humanity's treatment of one another to their treatment of him.

---

3. Rutledge, *Means of Grace*, 251.
4. Matt 25:31–33.
5. Rutledge, *Means of Grace*, 250.
6. Matt 25:40.

Underscoring the reality that all human acts are either glorifying God or are sins against him.

In God's grace, Jesus became human to feed the hungry, clothe the naked, and visit the sick and imprisoned. He fulfilled all the requirements needed to be a sheep. Having lived perfectly as a sheep, Jesus also names himself as the judge. He says to the Jewish leaders, "Moreover, the Father judges no one, but has entrusted all judgment to the Son."[7] The innocent sheep is also the judge, which makes the judge's character ideal. He has never taken a bribe, used his power to achieve selfish ends, or made a mistake in his judgements. He's never sent an innocent person to prison or let a guilty person go free. He is the perfect judge.

## JUSTICE IS THE FINAL WORD

The comfort of judgment is that God will bring all injustices to justice. The need for justice is as great as ever, and that is why it is good news that Jesus Christ will come to judge the living and the dead. We've been crying out for justice for as long as we've been around. Even the psalmist declares, "Lord, hear my just plea! Pay attention to my cry! Listen to my prayer, since it does not come from lying lips. Justice for me will come from your presence"[8] Only God can bring the ultimate justice we long for when we look around at our lives and the world and think, "God, why is life so unfair? Why do the innocent suffer and evil flourish? When will you answer our cries? When will you make all things right?" The world is out of sorts. We need God to put it right.

As a result of being a loving and merciful judge, he cannot stand the sight of any person being abused. Therefore, when we feel that disgust and rage boil up within us when we see photos of war zones or children abused, we can know that we feel only a tiny portion of what our judge feels about those egregious acts. Jesus' love compels him to not rest until the arc of history bends

---

7. John 5:22.
8. Ps 17:1–2.

toward justice. Because as Herman Bavinck writes, "All sin is absolutely opposed to the justice of God."[9] Therefore, sin must be vanquished in order for justice to reign.

The final day of justice is ultimately about God's vindication. When we neglect to love those in need, when we hurt those who are poor, we are neglecting and hurting God himself. So when we feel like God's judgment is too harsh, we have probably forgotten the nature of sin. As Herman Bavinck writes,

> God judges and punishes sin in accordance with its intrinsic quality. And that sin is infinite in the sense that it is committed against the highest majesty, who is absolutely entitled to our love and worship. God is absolutely and infinitely worthy of our obedience and dedication. . . . In the day of judgment . . . the issue is one of justice . . . the justice of God—that God himself may be honored as God in all eternity.[10]

It becomes evident regardless of how good a person is, no one can stand before this great God except himself because we have all sinned against him. He judges sin on its intrinsic quality, as a offense against God, rather than on how significant we believe it to be.

God's promised justice is comforting for those who are in Christ, but for those who are not in Christ, it is frightening. If any and every sin is tantamount to rebellion against the Creator God, then if he does not welcome us into his presence on the day of judgement, we will, as Jesus said, "go away to eternal punishment."[11] This is a difficult word from Jesus. Many Christians don't know how to reconcile God's judgment with the loving grace of Christ. We often think of people in our families or neighborhoods who don't profess belief in Jesus, but who are good people, generous, kind, and loving. We wonder, "Why would a loving God could condemn them to hell?" Yet, as I've laid out throughout this book, God's standard for judgment is not primarily about obeying his laws, although

---

9. Bavinck, *Holy Spirit*, 714.
10. Bavinck, *Holy Spirit*, 709–13.
11. Matt 25:46.

that is part of it, but rather it is about having no other gods before him. He demands our absolute love and devotion. If we do not give that to him, then we don't actually want to spend eternity with him. Instead, we already have chosen eternal separation from him. As Adam and Eve's original sin demonstrates, we want to be our own god. This is why a good neighbor, family member, or citizen can be brought before God's judgement and condemned. They've already chosen the path of condemnation.

Yet, for those who have thrown themselves at the feet of Jesus, God will actually praise us at the judgment instead of condemning us. He will rejoice over his children who have found themselves in his Son. God will celebrate our entrance into his presence like a father celebrating his prodigal son. The apostle Paul puts it this way, "He will bring to light what is hidden in darkness and will expose the motives of the heart. At that time each will receive their praise from God."[12] Praise from God is possible because it's not our motives that God will expose, but Jesus' motives on our behalf. The final piece of the Gospel's good news is that when judgment day comes, Jesus will again present himself before the Father on our behalf, and the Father will say, "Well done, my good and faithful servant."[13]

## CONCLUSION

C. S. Lewis's book *The Magician's Nephew* is the creation story of Narnia. It's similar and dissimilar to the creation story in the Bible. It's similar in that creation happens through words but is dissimilar in its form of speech. In Genesis, we read, "And God said, 'Let there be light,' and there was light."[14] A spoken word brought forth creation. However, in Narnia, Aslan doesn't just speak; he sings creation into existence. The narrator describes the song as,

---

12. 1 Cor 4:5.
13. Matt 25:21.
14. Gen 1:3.

A voice had begun to sing. It was very far away and Digory found it hard to decide from what direction it was coming. Sometimes it seemed to come from all directions at once. Sometimes he almost thought it was coming out of the earth beneath them. Its lower notes were deep enough to be the voice of the earth herself. There were no words. There was hardly even a tune. But it was, beyond comparison, the most beautiful noise he had ever heard. It was so beautiful he could hardly bear it.[15]

Although the biblical story doesn't begin with a song, it does end with one. Zephaniah prophesied Israel's restoration with these words: "The Lord your God is with you, the Mighty Warrior who saves. He will take great delight in you; in his love he will no longer rebuke you, but will rejoice over you with singing."[16] When all things are made new through Jesus Christ, God will sing a song over his people so beautiful we will hardly be able to bear it.

How could this Christian woman have made it through 101 years of life and believed that God was punishing her with leg pain because she had not amended all of her relationships? Lizzie's anxiety about God's judgment clouded her basic Christian understanding that God already poured out his judgment for sin upon Jesus Christ on the cross. When the Lord returns and we stand before the judgment seat, we will not receive what's due for our sins because Jesus has already received it in himself. Jesus himself says to look for redemption when he comes, not judgement: "At that time they will see the Son of Man coming in a cloud with power and great glory. When these things begin to take place, stand up and lift up your heads, because your redemption is drawing near."[17] He is the judge who declares the guilty verdict on himself instead of us, who are the perpetrators. Jesus says to us, "You are free now. Live for me!" We can wake up tomorrow free from anxiety about sin because we know that Jesus has taken sin's penalty upon himself. Therefore, we can freely confess our sins, stop hiding in

---

15. Lewis, *Magician's Nephew*, 106.
16. Zeph 3:17.
17. Luke 21:27–28.

shame and guilt, and seek to live a life marked by the grace and love of God. There may be earthly consequences to our sin, but we can rest assured knowing that the eternal consequences have been taken care of and nothing can take that away. The judgment is signed, sealed, and delivered.

# Conclusion: All Things Made New

*He came when all things were growing old, and made them new. As a made, created, perishing thing, the world was now declining to its fall. It could not but be that it should abound in troubles; He came both to console thee in the midst of present troubles, and to promise thee everlasting rest. Choose not then to cleave to this aged world, and to be unwilling to grow young in Christ.*

AUGUSTINE

AT THE BEGINNING OF this book, I mentioned my childhood pastor, Matt, and his wife, Mandy. Their journey of deconstruction led them to walk away from their faith in Jesus. It led them to doubt that the gospel offered any good news. Mandy even closed the podcast conversation by saying, "Spoiler alert, Jesus isn't coming back."[1] They don't feel like the gospel of Jesus offers satisfying enough answers to their many questions. I empathize with their plight. I still have many questions that feel unanswered. Yet, as you have journeyed with me in this book, I hope you have recognized that the gospel message isn't primarily about answering our questions. The gospel is about our mysterious relationship with the living God through Jesus Christ by the work of the Holy Spirit.

That said, we can know much about the mystery of faith. We can dive deep into the bottomless well of who God is, what he is

1. Mahon, *Slow Train*.

doing in this world, and why he has called us to Himself. We can explore the incredible wonder of salvation, the beauty of creation, and the endless journey of prayer. We need not shy away from tough questions; instead, we can bring them before our God, who loves us unconditionally and refuses to be himself without us. In Jesus, he pledges himself to us for all eternity, and that mission is not fulfilled until all things have been made new.

The good news of the gospel always concludes in the right place. As one of my parishioners once said after a Sunday sermon, "You don't always land your sermons in the right place, but today you did!" The gospel concludes with God's resounding yes to his creation. Instead of destroying this world forever, he promises to make everything new. Now that the incarnate Son of God sits at the Father's right hand in human flesh, he has provided the final guarantee of our eternal relationship. As a result, he will not abandon any aspect of his creation. Instead, he will destroy sin forever and show us what restored life with him is all about.

Over my years in ministry, Christians occasionally ask me what I think heaven will be like. My answer is always the same: heaven will be much like our lives now, yet without sin. Imagine a world where there are no abusive relationships, no unjust suffering, no hatred, or death. A wholesome life is the kind of life God has in store for us. A world permanently marked by peace, justice, love, and grace. The same Spirit that led Jesus to descend to earth will be the same Spirit that will flow through all people, and we will know joy in ways we cannot fathom.

This is no pie-in-the-sky theology. The hope of a new creation gives meaning to all our earthly attempts at justice, love, and mercy. The hope of the end is that God will not erase humanity from existence but will erase sin once and for all. All the ways that we perpetuate, experience, and encounter pain and suffering will end. What will remain will be the creation that God called *good*.

When we know the *telos*, or goal, of our lives and all of God's creation, we can experience lasting comfort in the present. It's like what Jayber Crow experiences when he looks at the river's surface near his home, in Wendell Berry's novel of the same name.

## Conclusion: All Things Made New

> The surface of the quieted river . . . is like a window looking into another world that is like this one except that it is quiet. Its quietness makes it seem perfect. The ripples are like the slats of a blind or a shutter through which we see imperfectly what is perfect. Though that other world can be seen only momentarily, it looks everlasting. As the ripples become more agitated, the window darkens and the other world is hidden. As I did not know then but know now, the surface of the river is like a living soul, which is easy to disturb, is often disturbed, but, growing calm, shows what it was, is, and will be.[2]

What window do we look through to see a world that brings hope? Does the promise of the next life bring us comfort, or does the coming judgement stir up fear? As the apostle Paul writes, "For now we see through a glass, darkly; but then face to face: now I know in part; but then shall I know even as also I am known."[3] By looking through that glass into the great unknown, we may only get a glimpse here and there, but as the future breaks into the present, it can create a sustainable life of faith, hope, and love. This future-oriented hope is the comfort we need amid a world of suffering.

What is most profound about the future is that God will dwell with his people. God's presence is the conclusion to his mission. As John writes in Rev 21:3-4, "And I heard a loud voice from the throne saying, 'Look! God's dwelling place is now among the people, and he will dwell with them. They will be his people, and God himself will be with them and be their God. "He will wipe every tear from their eyes. There will be no more death" or mourning or crying or pain, for the old order of things has passed away.'" There is no room for sin and death when God dwells with his people. God is our fullness; in him, we live, move, and have our being. The mystery of faith makes this divine and human relationship possible: Christ has died, Christ is risen, and Christ will come again.

---

2. Berry, *Jayber Crow*, 20.
3. 1 Cor 13:12 KJV.

# Bibliography

Allende, Isabel. *The Long Petal of the Sea*. New York: Ballantine, 2020.
Anglada, Maria Àngels. *The Violin of Auschwitz*. Translated by Martha Tennent. New York: Bantam, 2010.
Augustine. *Confessions*. Translated by Henry Chadwick. Oxford: Oxford University Press, 1991.
Balthasar, Hans Urs von. *Heart of the World*. San Francisco: Ignatius, 1980.
Barth, Karl. *Church Dogmatics*. 4/1: *The Doctrine of Reconciliation*. Edited by G. W. Bromiley and T. F. Torrance. Translated by G. W. Bromiley. New York: T&T Clark, 2004.
Bavinck, Herman. *Guidebook for Instruction in the Christian Religion*. Translated and edited by Gregory Parker Jr. and Cameron Clausing. Peabody, MA: Hendrickson, 2022.
———. *Holy Spirit, Church, and New Creation*. Vol. 4 of *Reformed Dogmatics*. Grand Rapids: Baker Academic, 2008.
———. *Sin and Salvation in Christ*. Vol. 3 of *Reformed Dogmatics*. Grand Rapids: Baker Academic, 2006.
Berry, Wendell. *Hannah Coulter: A Novel*. Washington, DC: Counterpoint, 2004.
———. *Jayber Crow: A Novel*. Washington, DC: Counterpoint, 2000.
———. *What Are People For? Essays*. Berkeley, CA: Counterpoint, 2010.
Brown, Brené. *Braving the Wilderness: The Quest for True Belonging and the Courage to Stand Alone*. New York: Random House, 2017.
———. *The Gifts of Imperfection: Let Go of Who You Think You're Supposed to Be and Embrace Who You Are*. Center City, MN: Hazelden, 2010.
Brueggemann, Walter. *Genesis*. Interpretation: A Bible Commentary for Teaching and Preaching. Atlanta: John Knox, 1982.
Buechner, Frederick. *A Crazy, Holy Grace: The Healing Power of Pain and Memory*. Grand Rapids: Zondervan, 2017.
Burge, Gary M. *John*. The NIV Application Commentary. Grand Rapids: Zondervan, 2000.
Buttrick, George Arthur. *Sermons Preached in a University Church*. Nashville: Abingdon, 1959.

# BIBLIOGRAPHY

Calvin, John. *Commentary on the First Book of Moses Called Genesis*, vol. 1. Translated by John King. Bellingham, WA: Faithlife, 2010.

———. *Institutes of the Christian Religion*. Translated by Henry Beveridge. Peabody, MA: Hendrickson, 2008.

Christian Reformed Church. "Heidelberg Catechism." Translated by Faith Alive Christian Resources, 2011. https://www.crcna.org/welcome/beliefs/confessions/heidelberg-catechism.

Doerr, Anthony. *Cloud Cuckoo Land*. New York: Simon & Schuster, 2021.

Dostoevsky, Fyodor. *Notes from a Dead House*. Translated by Richard Pevear and Larissa Volokhonsky. New York: Vintage Classics, 2015.

Frankl, Viktor E. *Man's Search for Meaning*. Boston: Beacon, 2006.

Gladwell, Malcolm. *David and Goliath: Underdogs, Misfits, and the Art of Battling Giants*. New York: Little, Brown, 2013.

Hannah, Kristin. *The Four Winds*. New York: St. Martin's, 2021.

Harari, Yuval Noah. *Sapiens: A Brief History of Humankind*. New York: Harper, 2015.

Hill, Wesley. *Easter: The Season of the Resurrection of Jesus*. Downers Grove, IL: InterVarsity, 2025.

Horton, Michael. *The Christian Faith: A Systematic Theology for Pilgrims on the Way*. Grand Rapids: Zondervan, 2011.

Keller, Tim. "Born into Hope." Gospel in Life, recorded Feb. 4, 2001. https://gospelinlife.com/sermon/born-into-hope/.

Lamott, Anne. *Somehow: Thoughts on Love*. New York: Riverhead, 2024.

———. "12 Truths I Learned from Life and Writing." Filmed Apr. 2017. TED video, 15:44. https://www.ted.com/talks/anne_lamott_12_truths_i_learned_from_life_and_writing?subtitle=en.

Lewis, C. S. *The Magician's Nephew*. New York: HarperCollins, 1955.

———. *The Four Loves*. New York: HarperOne, 2017.

Mahon, Josiah. *Slow Train to Heck*. Episode 42, "Love Really Does Win." Sept. 26, 2023. https://podcasts.apple.com/us/podcast/slow-train-to-heck/id1581431734?i=1000629290674.

McKnight, Scot. *1 Peter*. The NIV Application Commentary. Grand Rapids: Zondervan, 1996.

Mouw, Richard. *Adventures in Evangelical Civility: A Lifelong Quest for Common Ground*. Grand Rapids: Brazos, 2016.

Nevin, John Williamson. *The Mystical Presence: And the Doctrine of the Reformed Church on the Lord's Supper*. Eugene, OR: Wipf & Stock, 2012.

Noble, Alan. *You Are Not Your Own: Belonging to God in an Inhuman World*. Downers Grove, IL: InterVarsity, 2021.

Our World in Data. "Deaths per Year." 2024. https://ourworldindata.org/grapher/number-of-deaths-per-year.

Packer, J. I. *Concise Theology: A Guide to Historic Christian Beliefs*. Wheaton, IL: Tyndale House, 1993.

Peterson, Eugene H. *The Pastor: A Memoir*. New York: HarperOne, 2011.

# BIBLIOGRAPHY

Pevear, Richard. Introduction to *Notes from a Dead House*, by Fyodor Dostoevsky, translated by Richard Pevear and Larissa Volokhonsky, ix–xxix. New York: Vintage Classics, 2015.

Plantinga, Cornelius, Jr. *Not the Way It's Supposed to Be: A Breviary of Sin*. Grand Rapids: Eerdmans, 1995.

*Pyschology Today*. "Divorce." https://www.psychologytoday.com/us/basics/divorce.

Reeves, Michael. *Delighting in the Trinity: An Introduction to the Christian Faith*. Downers Grove, IL: IVP Academic, 2012.

Rutledge, Fleming. *Means of Grace: A Year of Weekly Devotions*. Grand Rapids: Eerdmans, 2020.

Schmemann, Alexander. *For the Life of the World: Sacraments and Orthodoxy*. New York: St. Vladimir's Seminary, 1997.

Smedes, Lewis B. *Love Within Limits: A Realist's View of 1 Corinthians 13*. Grand Rapids: Eerdmans, 1980.

Streep, Peg. "No, Parent-Child Estrangement Isn't Just a Fad." *Psychology Today*, May 20, 2023. https://www.psychologytoday.com/us/blog/tech-support/202305/no-adult-childparent-estrangement-isnt-a-fad.

Thiselton, Anthony C. *The First Epistle to the Corinthians: A Commentary on the Greek Text*. New International Greek Testament Commentary. Grand Rapids: Eerdmans, 2000.

Unkrich, Lee. *Toy Story 3*. Burbank, CA: Walt Disney Studios, 2010.

Williams, Rowan. *Being Christian: Baptism, Bible, Eucharist, Prayer*. Grand Rapids: Eerdmans, 2014.

Wiman, Christian. *My Bright Abyss: Meditation of a Modern Believer*. New York: Farrar, Straus & Giroux, 2013. Kindle.

Winston, Robert, and Rebecca Chicot. "The Importance of Early Bonding on the Long-Term Mental Health and Resilience of Children." *London Journal of Primary Care* 8.1 (Feb. 24, 2016) 12–14. https://doi.org/10.1080/17571472.2015.1133012.

Wright, N. T. *For All God's Worth: True Worship and the Calling of the Church*. Grand Rapids: Eerdmans, 1997.

Made in United States
Cleveland, OH
31 May 2025

17403247R00066